The Unbalanced Recovery

The Unbalanced Recovery

PETER ROBINSON
The London School of Economics

Philip Allan
OXFORD AND NEW JERSEY

First published 1988 by

PHILIP ALLAN PUBLISHERS LIMITED

Market Place   and   171 First Avenue
Deddington   Atlantic Highlands
Oxford OX5 4SE   New Jersey 07716
(UK)   (USA)

British Library Cataloguing in Publication Data
Robinson, Peter
  The unbalanced recovery.
  1. Great Britain—Economic policy—1945—
  I. Title
  330.941'0858   HC256.6

Library of Congress Cataloging in Publication Data
Robinson, Peter (Peter Raymond)
  The Unbalanced Recovery

  Bibliography: p
  Includes Index
  1. Unemployment—Great Britain. 2. Unemployment—
  Government Policy—Great Britain. 3. Unemployment—
  England—Cleveland. 4. Great Britain—Economic Policy.
  5. Great Britain—Economic Conditions—1945—
  I. Title
  HD5765.A6R635 1988 331.13'7941 88-2499

ISBN 0 86003 078 4
ISBN 0 86003 181 0 (pbk)

Set by MHL Typesetting Ltd, Coventry
Printed and bound in Great Britain by Antony Rowe Ltd, Chippenham

Contents

Introduction

'The beginning of wisdom is the admission of one's own lack of knowledge.'   E.F. Schumacher

In the early 1980s the British economy plunged into its most severe post-war recession, when nearly two million jobs were lost and unemployment almost trebled. Since about 1983 there has been something of a recovery in economic growth and in employment, though unemployment has remained stubbornly high. However, this recovery has been seriously unbalanced in two main respects: it has left behind certain communities and it has by-passed people who have been out of work for a long time — the long-term unemployed. In the first part of this book I will try to explain why these imbalances have arisen. In doing so I am going to draw on some evidence from the experience of Cleveland County in the north-east of England, which has declined from being a 1960s growth zone to become one of Britain's most serious economic blackspots.

In trying to learn some lessons by looking at a case study of how one area has been affected by economic change in the past two decades, this book is somewhat unusual when compared with the standard kind of text written by economists. Economics has always tried to be a 'universal' social science, in that it attempts to construct theories of human behaviour which are supposed to be relevant to all places and all times. A piece of work written by an American economist in the confines of a college in Cleveland, Ohio, is supposed to contain some truths which are also applicable to Cleveland, England. This is the first reason why modern economics can often seem impersonal and obscure, because very rarely do economists try to write their thoughts with reference to one specific community. Even in those chapters in the book where Cleveland

(England) is not mentioned, I have tried to bear in mind that whatever I have written ought to make some sense when considered in the context of my home county. The increase in the attention paid to pure theory in the economics profession probably results from the fact that few economists ever ask whether what they are writing really makes sense when considered from the point of view of the grass roots.

Another question which is rarely asked is whether what is being written is really intelligible to individuals who are not expert economists and who do not understand the jargon and techniques being used by the profession. Modern economics is becoming relentlessly technical, to the extent that it is cutting itself off from the real world. Economists usually communicate only with each other and rarely with outsiders. This is a pity, because it means that even research which is highly relevant to what is going on in the real world gets ignored because it is written in such a fashion as to be inaccessible. Politicians who pick up bits and pieces of the subject usually seem to absorb only the worst or the most out-of-date elements. At times the profession appears to be equally divided between the work which is irrelevant because it refuses to address the real world, and the work which is relevant, but is not communicated properly to non-economists, or does not fit into the prejudices of the policy makers.

The London School of Economics reflects many of these problems. Firstly, it has been suggested that LSE really stands for 'London and the South-East', in that the institution is dominated by the perceptions of the capital, but has little sympathy for looking at any problem from the point of view of a location 'north of Watford'. The research bodies associated with the LSE are located on the fourth floor of the library building, but this floor cannot be reached from the rest of the building. Access to the researchers is via an obscure side entrance whose location is rarely revealed to the undergraduates. It is almost as if the research bodies have deliberately tried to isolate themselves physically from the rest of the world. The research seminars cater for a restricted inner circle of academics, civil servants and graduate students.

It is not clear that this is what the Fabians had in mind when they founded the LSE at the turn of the century. I think the idea was to try to sponsor research which would be directly relevant in helping to resolve some of the world's economic, social and political problems, and to be relevant it had to be understandable and it had to be sensitive to the impact of these problems on individuals and the communities in which they lived. Modern economics now rarely considers the importance of history, institutions, or culture, and certainly never takes into account the influence of individuals on economic problems and the impact of those problems on individuals. Indeed, economics proceeds from the abstract notion that, essentially, each person is the same and is driven by the same motivations. It is left to others to consider the individual.

This book, then, has been partly motivated by a certain dissatisfaction with the direction taken by the economics profession in recent decades. Consistent with this are the two value judgements which underlie much of what is written. Firstly, there is a principle of economic justice — that any government, institution or policy should be evaluated on the basis of what it achieves for those individuals who have the fewest innate advantages. Secondly, in responding to any problem, the policy makers ought to pay close attention to the views of those individuals most affected by the problem. It will be suggested time and again that people have a right to own their own problems and to have an input into the solutions proffered.

Chapter 1 offers a structure of analysis for looking at Britain's economic problems, so that everything which is discussed in this book can be placed in some kind of context. The chapter also outlines a set of criteria by which we might judge any policy which has the aim of reducing unemployment. This chapter deals with some difficult ideas, but although I think it is important to look at major questions from the point of view of local communities, it is also important not to lose touch with the wider picture. Chapter 2 introduces the reader to Cleveland County and the traumas of recent years and also offers a critique of traditional regional policy. Chapter 3 develops the theme of 'the unbalanced recovery' and is followed by a chapter which tries to relate what we know about the consequences of long-term unemployment.

The next few chapters look at the policy response of the present government to the existence of these severe imbalances in economic prosperity. Chapter 5 considers the case for trying to make market forces work more effectively. Chapter 6, by contrast, looks at the increasing state intervention in the inner cities and problem regions, while in the following chapter we look at the growth in the programmes of the Manpower Services Commission, which has become the government's chief instrument for tackling unemployment. Chapter 8 looks at some of the labour market and regional policies in operation in Sweden and in the United States. Chapter 9 explores the growing involvement of local authorities in economic development and addresses the issues raised by policies directed towards the creation of new small businesses.

The last third of the book explores some ideas for trying to counter the unbalanced recovery. Chapter 10 suggests ways in which the private sector might be persuaded to tilt its recruitment and location practices, and Chapter 11 explores how the provision of public sector services might be reformed to make them more relevant to local communities and more capable of generating employment for those who are the most disadvantaged in the labour market. Chapter 12 looks at the reform of education and training, a contentious but vitally important subject, and the final chapter looks at some political and institutional reforms which are necessary if a serious attack on the unbalanced recovery is to be mounted.

The scope of issues covered is, I think, very wide. I hope this breadth of treatment is not at the expense of depth; I think it is more useful than a focus on one single and very narrow subject. The aspiration to steer clear of unfamiliar jargon and techniques has, I hope, been fulfilled, and the style of the book is very much aimed at an audience of non-economists, who nevertheless would like to learn what on earth is going on in the British economy. To the extent that there are gaps or inconsistencies in the argument, this will reflect the fact that the book was completed in four months and by someone who has never attempted this kind of thing before.

Despite the earlier unkind remarks about the LSE, this book would not have been written without the backing of Richard Layard who, even though he disagrees with a lot of it, has been gentlemanly enough to help me get it published. Thanks are also due to the staff at the Centre for Labour Economics, especially Suzie, who typed the manuscript, and Marion, Ellen, Joanne and Phyllis, the other secretaries who do all the really hard work for which the rest of us take the credit. Jonathan Haskel read some of the text and I appreciate the friendship shown by Andrew Oswald, even though he probably won't agree with a word that's written here!

Debts are also due to Fred Robinson and his colleagues at the Centre for Urban and Regional Development Studies at Newcastle University and to the staff at the Centre for Local Research at Teesside Polytechnic. Thank you also to Eric Smith and his colleagues at Cleveland County Council and to Geoff Garnett at the Manpower Services Commission in Middlesbrough, and to the many other individuals I met while conducting this research. A final thanks to Nigel Brearley who read the text and kept up my morale.

The Problem

1
The Economics of Unemployment

'Any fool can deflate the economy and any fool can launch an inflationary boom. The art lies in balancing a whole series of desirable, but sometimes conflicting, objectives.'[1]

Mrs Thatcher's Government came to office in May 1979 determined to reverse Britain's economic misfortunes and restore its prosperity. To understand the course of events since 1979 we must understand the strategy which lay behind this determination and to understand its impact we must first explore precisely what we mean by our economic misfortunes.

It is not often recognised that Britain's economic problem is essentially twofold (Figure 1.1 — and no apologies for the complexity of the diagram — is meant to illustrate the complexity of our problems). Since the last quarter of the last century, productivity growth in the United Kingdom has lagged behind that of our major competitors (Table 1.1). This has become more readily noticeable since the end of the Second World War when these nations caught up and passed the United Kingdom in terms of productivity levels. This process is best seen as a long-distance race between athletes. Britain was given a head start of one lap by virtue of being the first to industrialise. The United States was second off the block and, by the outbreak of the First World War at the latest, was stealing Britain's first place. The other nations were later in getting started (Italy was last), but they too have gradually caught Britain up (Italy probably during this decade). This is what has become known as the 'British Disease', although calling it the 'Anglo-Saxon Disease' might be more appropriate since, from the 1950s, productivity growth in the United States has been very poor, so that the other industrialised nations of the West have begun to catch up with America, too.

3

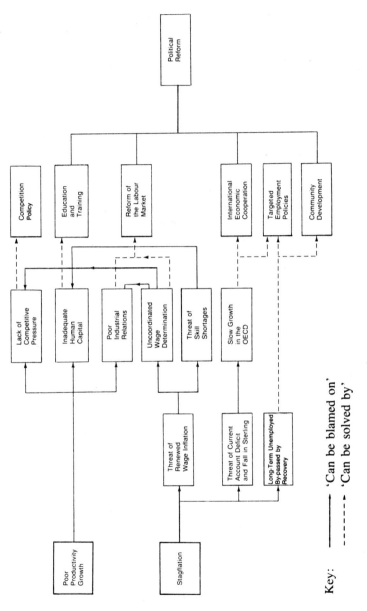

Figure 1.1 Britain's Economic Malaise: A Structure for Analysis

Key: ——————— 'Can be blamed on'

        - - - - - - ▶ 'Can be solved by'

Table 1.1 Growth Rates of Real GDP per Person Employed (Average Annual Percentage)

	1873–1899	1899–1913	1913–1950	1950–1973	1973–1979	1979–1983	1983–1986
United States	1.9	1.3	1.7	2.2	0.2	0.2	1.1
Japan	1.1	1.8	1.7	7.8	2.9	2.6	2.5
West Germany	1.5	1.5	0.6	4.6	3.0	1.3	2.1
France	1.3	1.6	0.9	4.4	2.9	1.4	2.0
Italy	0.3	2.5	0.9	5.5	1.6	0.5	2.1
United Kingdom	1.2	0.5	0.6	2.5	1.2	2.1	1.6
Canada	1.9	1.9	1.0	2.8	0.5	n.a.	1.4
Sweden	1.5	2.1	1.4	3.0	0.5	0.9	n.a.

The second great problem of the British economy has been given the unlovely name of 'stagflation' and is the simultaneous occurrence of both high inflation and high unemployment. Two factors distinguish 'stagflation' from the 'British Disease'. The first is time scale: the beginnings of stagflation date from the late 1960s, while the British Disease has its roots in the late nineteenth century.[2] Secondly, stagflation has affected *all* of the industrialised nations of the West to a greater or lesser extent, although it has to be admitted that Britain has had one of the worst performances (Table 1.2). Of course there have been many occasions in the past (of which the Great Depression of the inter-war period is most familiar) when unemployment has exploded to serious proportions, but the past twenty years is the first time that the industrialised world as a whole has witnessed both serious unemployment and serious inflation.

What have been the causes of these two problems? If we turn first to our poor rate of productivity growth we can identify three major causes (though this is not to deny that other, minor, factors may have been at work). As we shall explore more closely in Chapter 12, it has been recognised for some 120 years that the primary cause of our falling behind in the productivity race is an inadequate investment in the education and training of the British people or, in the jargon, inadequate human capital. A second problem has been the poor state of industrial relations in Britain, particularly in the larger manufacturing establishments. Finally, many commentators have pointed to the lack of internal competitive pressures, with large domestic firms unwilling to compete fiercely in the domestic market (in contrast to Japan, for example) and the equal lack of external competitive pressures, at least before membership of the European Community, when the tying of British firms to more or less protected imperial markets finally came to an end.[3]

To understand the causes of stagflation is to understand the government's economic strategy and to understand stagflation one needs to look closely at the British labour market.

The economic strategy of the government, crudely labelled 'monetarism', was based on very simple principles. The underlying cause of high unemployment was taken to be high inflation which, it was argued, undermined Britain's competitiveness and reduced individuals' incentives to save and firms' incentives to invest. The underlying cause of inflation was too fast a rate of growth of the money supply. The answer: restrict the rate of monetary growth, gradually reduce inflation, and 'eventually' unemployment will come down to its 'natural' rate. Unfortunately, 'eventually' seems to be taking a long time. Of course,

Table 1.2 Economic Performance in 8 OECD Countries (1973–86)

	Average unemployment rate 1973–79	Average inflation rate 1973–79	Average unemployment rate 1980–86	Average inflation rate 1980–86	Long-term unemployment as a proportion of total unemployment, 1984
United States	6.4	8.2	7.9	5.8	12.3
Canada	6.9	7.7	9.9	8.6	9.9
Japan	1.8	10.4	2.5	2.9	15.2
France	4.2	10.2	8.6	11.6	42.3
West Germany	2.9	5.0	6.8	4.2	32.7
Italy	6.5	15.3	9.3	18.1	41.9
United Kingdom	5.1	14.8	11.1	8.3	39.8
Sweden	2.0	11.4	3.0	9.8	12.3
Average	4.5	10.4	7.4	8.7	25.8

the government recognised that there would be some transitory unemployment, but the scale and duration of unemployment in Britain in the 1980s does genuinely seem to have taken the government by surprise. Indeed, this explains much of the rest of this book, for the growth in the programmes of the Manpower Services Commission (Chapter 7), and the proliferation in the 'alphabet agencies' devoted to urban and regional regeneration (Chapter 6) reflect the almost 'panic' response of a government which seriously underestimated the results for unemployment of its original strategy.

The failure, or at least incomplete success, of the government's strategy is in fact the outcome of ignoring the most simple rule in macroeconomics: you must have at least as many policy instruments to match your policy targets.[4] Tackling stagflation means reducing both high inflation and high unemployment: two targets, and they require two instruments. At best, the government has had only one and a half instruments: its financial policy (monetary and fiscal controls which can be used to determine the path of nominal demand), and a very imperfect labour market policy which has consisted of a gradual programme of trade union reform and equally gradual measures to deregulate the bottom half of the British labour market (for example, by relaxing the rules governing the wages councils).

It is also true that the government's original strategy was essentially illogical. If high inflation causes high unemployment mainly by undermining British industry's competitiveness, what is the logic in driving down inflation with a monetary policy which works via a high real exchange rate which reduces inflation, but which also undermines our competitiveness and increases unemployment?

The Callaghan Government had a financial policy which was not very different from the policy followed by the first Thatcher administration from 1979 to 83. 'Monetarism' dates from the intervention of the IMF in 1976. However, this was combined with an incomes policy which was, in its initial phase, highly successful in helping to reduce inflation without vastly increased unemployment.[5] Of course, this incomes policy broke down in the winter of 1978/79, so that from 1979 to 83 financial policy was almost on its own in fighting stagflation. One instrument can only hit one target (inflation) and the second (unemployment) can only be sacrificed.

Since 1983, the government can claim the creation of over one million jobs and since June 1986 it can claim that unemployment has been falling

(Chapter 3 will investigate these trends in more detail). This is not, however, a vindication of government strategy, but rather an indication that the government's financial policy has been slowly dismantled in its original form. The commitment to reduce government expenditure in real terms has been replaced by the commitment to hold it constant and, from autumn 1986, to hold its growth to 1½ per cent a year. Monetary targets have been effectively abandoned, credit allowed to grow, and sterling heavily devalued against the currencies of our major competitors (especially the German Mark). The rapid build-up in consumer spending also reflects the growth of wages far in advance of prices, which is an indication of the failure of the government's labour market strategy. The fall in unemployment from mid-1986 says more about the increasing activities of the MSC and a significant relaxation of financial policy than about the success of the government's original strategy.

Interesting comparisons can be drawn with the United States. Reaganomics Mark I was very similar to Mrs Thatcher's 1979–83 strategy (although October 1979 is the better watershed for the US, when the Federal Reserve adopted monetary targeting). Since 1982/83, an increase in Federal expenditure on defence and a gradual relaxation of monetary policy, combined with massive tax cutting, have served to deliver an enormous fiscal and monetary boost to the US economy — Reaganomics Mark II. Financial policy in Britain since 1983 has been a pale imitation of this.

It has been only a very pale imitation because of the perceived problems of trying to go as far as the United States. By definition, unemployment can only fall if the rate of growth of actual output is faster than the rate of growth of potential output (which is given by the growth of productivity and the labour force). In the United States, actual output has grown very strongly (especially in 1984) while productivity has been sluggish (although labour force growth has been quite strong). In Britain, since 1983, we have registered growth rates averaging 3 per cent per annum, but this has only just matched the growth in productivity and the labour force. Actual output would need to grow by at least 4 per cent a year for any substantial reduction in unemployment. This is precisely what has occurred in 1986–7: output has grown at an annual rate of 4 per cent and unemployment has fallen significantly.

Before 1986–87 actual output was not allowed to grow faster than 4 per cent a year because of the twin fears of a deterioration in the current account of the balance of payments, a sharp fall in sterling and a burst of imported inflation, and the threat of renewed wage inflation (Figure 1.1). It is at this point that the causes of stagflation and the causes of the British Disease begin to inter-relate. The key problem of our labour market is the uncoordinated process of wage determination which can be partly related to poor industrial relations and is compounded by a lack of competitive pressure. In addition there is the threat of possible future skill shortages which blends with our emphasis on inadequate investment in human capital as a fundamental cause of poor productivity growth.

Any attempt to boost output growth in the UK may well fail unless other countries (especially Germany and Japan) also stimulate their economies, but at present the political will to coordinate macroeconomic policy at the international level is sadly lacking.

At the domestic level, what we still lack is a full instrument of labour market strategy. The present government approach is failing because it is aimed at the lower half of the labour market, whereas it appears to be in the top half of the income distribution range that inflationary wage trends are being set.[6] The answer lies in a tax-based or other form of incomes policy, and a whole plethora of other reforms needed in the structure of industrial relations in this country.

The final problem we need to address, and which forms the heart of this book, is the very unbalanced nature of the present recovery in employment, which seems to be largely by-passing the long-term unemployed (those out of work for twelve months or more) and other disadvantaged labour market groups. Even if we could boost output growth significantly, it is not at all certain that the long-term unemployed (LTU) would benefit. The key argument of this book is that any measure designed to boost output and employment must be very carefully targeted towards those unemployed who have the least chance of finding jobs on their own. Moreover, as we shall argue that it is often entire communities which can get by-passed by what economic recovery does take place, there is a powerful case for encouraging action within these very communities so that people can grasp for themselves some influence over their future.

When we tie all these factors together, we have a seven-point strategy for dealing with Britain's economic malaise: (1) an increase in competitive pressures in both the internal and external markets; (2) a quite fundamental reform of our system of education and training; (3) the reform of the labour market; (4) an attempt to secure a better coordination of the economic policies of individual nations; (5) employment policies carefully targeted at the LTU; and (6) measures to give individual communities more control over their future. The seventh part of this strategy is the political reforms which would be required at the local, national and international level to implement the first six elements of the strategy, and some discussion of this takes place in our concluding chapter. Essentially, this book is concerned with points 2, 5, 6, and 7 of the strategy — labour market reform, international cooperation and competition policy would require books in themselves.

How does the administration of Mrs Thatcher, 1979−87, measure up to this proposed strategy? Competition policy has largely become synonymous with privatisation and we have a few things to say about this in Chapter 11. The government has awoken very late to the need to reform education and training (Chapters 7 and 12). We have already hinted that its labour market strategy is seriously weak in several respects. Its attitude to international cooperation could best be described as one of polite indifference, if not contempt. Its employment policies are very poorly targeted and its attitude to community initiatives and political reform is often downright hostile: the government does not score high marks.

We continue to have one of the worst performances in both inflation and unemployment among the eight industrial countries in Table 1.2. As for productivity, although there was a short breakthrough in 1979−83 reflecting the rapid scrapping of inefficient plant, it remains unproven whether this can be sustained. Interestingly, since 1984 the group of eight nations appears to have reverted to the pre-1973 pattern of productivity growth, with Britain ahead of only Canada and the United States (Table 1.1).

How to Judge Employment Policies

There is a whole range of policies aimed at reducing unemployment in operation in the British economy and many policy alternatives are offered by critics of the present government. What we need is a consistent set of criteria by which we might judge both the existing and the proposed policies, and this is what we are going to try to outline below. The criteria we have picked reflect our interpretation of what constitutes Britain's economic malaise, and are not exhaustive. If the reader disagrees with the criteria, he should offer an alternative set, but the substantive point is that we should aim to judge all policies on a consistent basis as this is the only fair way to distinguish between them. So here we go with our simple six-point check list for judging programmes which have been proposed as ways to reduce unemployment:

(1) They should be capable of being targeted upon the long-term unemployed (LTU) and other disadvantaged labour market groups — they should not therefore demand an unnecessarily unrealistic level of skills (or should offer further education and training so the LTU can acquire the necessary skills).

(2) They should be cost-effective, involving as small a rise in net public spending as is feasible.

(3) They should offer some wider community benefit, producing output which is socially valuable.

(4) They should be capable of being organised on a reasonable time scale.

(5) They should have the lowest impact feasible on inflation. This can be assured firstly by targeting the jobs on the LTU and so avoiding pressure in the labour market (see below), and secondly by targeting sectors with a low propensity to import, so avoiding balance of payments and exchange rate difficulties.

(6) They should raise the chances of participants securing permanent employment if the scheme offered is only temporary (as is the case with the programmes organised by the Manpower Services Commission).

Of these criteria, the first one is by far the most important, for the key argument which is presented in the first part of this book is that those individuals who have been out of work for a long time are being by-passed by the unbalanced economic recovery, and any unemployment policy must be judged firstly on how it contributes to countering this imbalance. The second criterion is the one that has up until now been dominant, both in government circles and amongst their critics. However, excessive focus on short-run costs can be misleading for it diverts attention from an analysis of the long-run benefits to be derived from a programme. The economist is likely to focus on the third criterion, bearing in mind Lord Keynes' old joke about getting the unemployed to dig holes and then fill them in again as a solution to the Great Depression. When there is so much unfulfilled need in the country we should not squander resources on programmes which deliver an output of dubious social value. This is a wider definition of efficiency than focusing on cost-effectiveness alone.

The fourth criterion is there to guard against the proposals for vast, grandiose constructions designed to create employment, but which would take five years to plan and therefore seem less attractive as a means of tackling the problem which is here and now. The sixth criterion is specifically aimed at temporary programmes. Participants on MSC schemes judge them first and foremost on whether they raise their chances of obtaining a decent job which is likely to last for a reasonable period, and what participants fear most is a spell on a scheme followed by an immediate return to the dole queue.

The fifth criterion is perhaps the most difficult one. As the quote at the begining of the chapter recognised, we do not want to swap high unemployment for a re-acceleration of inflation, and it would be rather nice to avoid both. There is now a body of argument which suggests that the long-term unemployed are playing no role in holding down inflation.

Conventional economic theory asserts that a high level of unemployment ought to reduce significantly the rate of wage inflation and therefore the rate of price inflation. However, since 1983, the rate of wage inflation has been stuck at about 7½ per cent per annum and shows no signs of either falling or rising significantly, and this despite three million people out of work. This phenomenon has brought forth a torrent of research by various economists, although it would have to be admitted that there exists only a very limited consensus as to what are the main reasons for this state of affairs.

Nevertheless, there are a number of studies which do suggest that because the long-term unemployed have become detached from the labour market, they are no longer doing their 'job' of holding down inflation.[7] One can certainly find some good reasons for accepting this argument. Employers may be suspicious of people who have been out of work for a long time because their skills (or their work habits) may have eroded. In deciding on the wages which they intend to offer, they may pay attention only to their existing employees, trends in other firms, and the possibility of recruiting people who have been out of work for a short time. The trade unions are likewise most naturally concerned with their existing members and the long-term unemployed tend, almost without exception, to drop out of their unions.

There are at least two particularly influential econometric studies which provide backing for the thesis that the long-term unemployed play no role in checking wage inflation.[8] However, there are equivalent studies which do not support this thesis[9] and for those of us who are unwilling or unable to comment upon such complex work it is wise to defer judgement. One problem is the definition of long-term unemployment, usually taken to mean that a person has been out of work for over one year. An individual who participates, if only for a few weeks, in a scheme organised by the MSC and then leaves to rejoin the dole queue is then classified as short-term unemployed and is presumed therefore to be joining the fight against inflation. However, as we shall show in Chapter 7, it is by no means proven that a period on, for example, the Community Programme, implies that an individual is thereby in a position to exert competitive pressure in the labour market. It is also interesting that in Belgium and Holland long-term unemployment is significantly worse than in Britain, but wage inflation has nevertheless collapsed.

It would be unwise, then, to overstress the importance of the theory that the LTU play no role in reducing inflation and that employment programmes aimed at them would have no inflationary effect whatsoever. Our more circumspect conclusions follow those of one of the influential studies quoted earlier in that 'we do not accept the extreme view (that the long-term unemployed have no effect on wage increases) but we certainly accept that the potential consequences for inflation are much less severe if job-creation schemes are directed at the long-term unemployed.'[10] This means that very carefully targeted programmes can only be one part of a wider strategy and that policies directed at the labour market and the exchange rate cannot be neglected.

To illustrate the utility of our criteria it is quite useful to look in some detail at the case for cuts in the standard rate of income tax, which form a central part of the government's strategy. The first thing to say is that all the major models of the British economy are unanimous in rejecting income-tax cuts on the basis of our second criterion, for cuts in the basic rate are the least cost-effective way of boosting demand and creating employment. The Treasury's own model of the British economy would suggest that the net cost per job created through income-tax cuts is £46,900, which is more than five times as expensive as carefully targeted increases in current public expenditure, four times as expensive as certain types of capital repair and renovation, and more than twice as expensive as cuts in employers' national insurance contributions. Only cuts in VAT are as ineffective.[11] The National Institute model suggests that income tax cuts '. . . are a relatively ineffective instrument . . .' for reducing unemployment, and the London Business School model also confirms '. . . the conventional view that cuts in income tax are a relatively ineffective means of expanding demand.'[12] In fact, the degree of unanimity on this issue is surprising given the reputation that economists have acquired for never agreeing on anything. The economists' defence might be that even when they do agree, if the conclusions are unpalatable to the politicians, the profession will still be completely ignored.

However, we have argued that looking purely at the issue of cost-effectiveness is too limiting, so how does the case for income-tax cuts score on our other criteria? The government and its intellectual supporters would argue that income-tax cuts have a significant effect on increasing incentives to work and the willingness to take risks, which would fall under our third criterion in being a long-run social benefit. Fortunately, we now have the results of the Treasury's own exhaustive study on this supply-side issue, conducted by Charles Brown of Stirling University, which suggests that those who would work more hours under the stimulus of a reduction in the standard rate of income tax are exactly counterbalanced by those who would use the opportunity to increase their leisure time.[13] There is absolutely no evidence available for the impact of income tax on the willingness to accept risk.[14]

Increases in government expenditure work far more quickly in expanding demand than income-tax cuts, which thus fail our fourth criterion. There is no econometrically robust evidence that cuts in income tax reduce wage inflation by boosting workers' post-tax incomes[15] and those income groups which have seen most benefit from cuts in direct taxes since 1979 have also had the fastest rate of inflation in their wages. Income-tax cuts, which feed through into higher consumer expenditure, are about twice as likely to suck in imports as carefully targeted public expenditure.[16] The London Business School and National Institute models both confirm that income-tax cuts are significantly more inflationary than targeted public expenditure, so that tax cuts fail our fifth criterion.

Even if the reader is not impressed that income-tax cuts have so far failed four out of six criteria (with the sixth not relevant here), he should consider our first and most important criterion. By definition, income-tax cuts cannot be targeted on the long-term unemployed who are not paying tax anyway and there is not one shred of evidence that boosting the incomes of those in work creates a 'trickle-down' effect which benefits those out of work.

Income-tax cuts benefit those who are already doing best out of the economy while reinforcing the marginalisation of those who are being by-passed by the unbalanced recovery, and it is the failure of tax cuts to pass this test which ought to be stressed above all.

If income-tax cuts are a very poor instrument for reducing unemployment, how do some of the government's other policies score, and what alternatives can we suggest? The second and third parts of the book deal with these questions. First, we should define more clearly what we mean by the unbalanced recovery and what we might learn about it by looking at individual communities.

Notes

1. An anonymous member of Mrs Thatcher's Cabinet as quoted in Cornwall (1983), p. 245.
2. See Dahrendorff (1982) for the argument for taking the late 19th century as the watershed in Britain's productivity growth in relation to our competitors.
3. The three factors emphasised here in explaining Britain's relatively poor productivity growth come from the two most exhaustive studies of British relative productivity, namely Prais, *et al.* (1981) and Caves and Davies (1987).
4. This is the famous Tinbergen rule, named after the Dutch economist who first stressed its importance. In effect it means that if you aim one arrow at two targets simultaneously, you miss both. It is common sense, like most good economics.
5. See Wadhwani (1985) which, in common with other econometric studies, suggests that the Social Contract of 1975–77 was the only successful incomes policy of the post-war period in the UK.
6. This is most persuasively argued in Nickell (1986).
7. An excellent introduction to this argument is provided in Layard (1986) and Jackman (1986).
8. See Layard and Nickell in Bean, Layard and Nickell (eds) (1987), and Budd, Levine and Smith (1987).
9. See, for example, Carruth and Oswald (1986).
10. Budd, Levine and Smith (1987). This article follows on from previous work.
11. See *Charter for Jobs Economic Report*, March 1987, vol. 2, no. 6. The simulations on the Treasury model were performed by the House of Commons Parliamentary Unit at the University of Warwick. Similar results using the Treasury model are reported by the Policy Research Institue at Leeds

Polytechnic (*New Society*, 8 May 1987). See also Davies and Metcalf (1985) and Standing (1986).

12. See London Business School, *Economic Outlook, 1986—90*, vol. 11, no. 5, February 1987, and National Institute *Economic Review*, February 1987.
13. Brown's earlier results are available as Brown (1981). The LSE's Mervyn King believes that high marginal tax rates over 50 per cent may be counter-productive but this is an entirely separate argument from reducing the standard rate.
14. See Atkinson and Stiglitz (1980).
15. Davies and Metcalf (1985).
16. Davies and Metcalf (1985).

2
Cleveland: A Suitable Case
for Treatment

'The nature of society on Teesside was dominated by the two great big employers. People were used to cradle-to-the-grave employment. The only choice was whether you worked for BSC or ICI.'[1]

The secret to visiting the County of Cleveland lies in travelling by road rather than by rail. The railway journey from Darlington to Middlesbrough and on to Redcar is one of the most dispiriting experiences one can imagine, especially in the latter stages when the line passes through derelict land, redundant docks, heaving steelworks and slum housing. If you had arrived with a set of prejudices about the dirty, depressed North, you might feel justified in having them confirmed.

Cleveland consists of four boroughs, three of which (Langbaurgh, Middlesbrough and Stockton) constitute the conurbation of Teesside to which, in 1974, was added the Borough of Hartlepool.[2] The county is a classic example of mid-Victorian industrialisation based on the coking coal of South Durham and the iron ore of the Cleveland Hills. Stockton was the terminus of Stephenson's famous railway line from Darlington, opened in 1825, and Middlesbrough was a purpose-built port and iron and steel town constructed in the middle of the nineteenth century.[3] The area suffered greatly from the inter-war depression and only recovered during the great period of rearmament in the late 1930s which reinforced the traditional patterns of economic activity by boosting demand in the iron and steel, shipbuilding, and engineering industries.[4] The only sign of diversification was the beginnings of ICI's huge contribution to the local economy when its first plant opened at Billingham, north of the River Tees, in 1923, to be followed after 1945 by the huge two-thousand-acre petrochemicals complex at Wilton near Redcar.

However, it would be entirely misleading to paint a caricature of

18

Cleveland as being a typical depressed area of the North, and the railway journey described above is interesting precisely because it gives an unbalanced and unfair portrait of the county. The area as a whole has more than its fair share of social and economic problems, to be sure, but it also has much pleasant housing, good schools and easy access to some of the most beautiful countryside in Britain. However, as we shall explore in the next chapter, it is the *perceived image* of a locality which is a crucial determinant of that area's prosperity, whatever the actual case might be.

The quote at the beginning of the chapter states an important truth about the county: its dominance by three industries (steel, heavy engineering, and chemicals) and two firms (British Steel and ICI). Teesside could justifiably claim the title of the Jewel in the Crown of the traditional regional policy of the 1960s and 1970s, when the two big employers (and other firms) poured many billions of pounds of investment into the area subsidised by the State in the form of automatic Regional Development Grants (RDGs). Indeed, during the mid-1970s, Cleveland was receiving fully one-quarter of all the RDG payments made in the whole of Britain. The BSC complex at Redcar was built as the largest integrated basic iron and steel plant in Europe, while ICI Wilton became one of Europe's greatest petrochemicals plants. It could not be argued, then, that Cleveland's problems are largely a function of past under-investment, for the county has a very capital-intensive manufacturing sector.[5] Indeed, before 1976, Teesside was more akin to the West Midlands in giving off an air of considerable prosperity and optimism, which now strikes those looking back as unjustified complacency.

Since 1976, employment in manufacturing and construction in the county has been halved, while public expenditure restraints have reduced public-sector job opportunities too, leaving only financial, business and miscellaneous services as very modest areas of growth (Table 2.1). There has been enormous shedding of labour in the steel and chemicals plants and wholesale closures of engineering establishments, with an annual average rate of net job loss in manufacturing of 5,700 per annum. The consequences have been an explosion in unemployment which has trebled since 1976 so that by the mid-1980s over one in five of the county's labour force was without a job, giving Cleveland the highest unemployment rate on a county basis in the mainland of Britain (Table 2.2).

How should we explain this haemorrhage of jobs? The greatest period of job loss occurred during the great 1979−81 recession when those parts of the economy most exposed to international competition suffered from

Table 2.1   Employment Trends in Cleveland, 1975—1986

Industry Group	1975	1978	1981	1984	1986
PRIMARY	4,800	5,000	5,500	5,400	5,300
Oil and chemicals	27,900	28,600	22,600	19,100	18,700
Metal manufacturing	28,100	25,200	18,200	11,200	10,900
Mechanical engineering & shipbuilding	18,100	12,900	8,900	6,900	6,900
Other manufacturing	31,400	26,800	21,400	19,100	18,600
ALL MANUFACTURING	105,500	93,500	71,100	56,300	55,100
CONSTRUCTION	22,700	22,200	14,100	12,100	11,600
Transport	13,300	12,800	11,900	11,500	11,500
Distribution	25,800	28,100	24,700	24,900	24,900
Financial, business & misc. services	28,100	34,900	33,800	34,100	35,200
Health, education & public administration	45,300	38,700	39,200	38,100	38,300
ALL SERVICES	112,500	114,500	109,600	108,600	109,900
TOTAL EMPLOYEES	245,500	235,200	200,300	182,400	181,900

the drastic loss in competitiveness which was a result of the explosion of domestic wage inflation and the overvaluation of the pound against the world's other currencies. This factor is particularly important in explaining the massive rationalisation of employment in ICI where the number of jobs collapsed from a peak of 25,000 in 1976 to 14,000 ten years later. BSC was caught in a double squeeze on employment, with

Table 2.2 Unemployment in Cleveland and the United Kingdom, 1973—1987

	Cleveland		United Kingdom	
	Number	%	Number	%
1973	12,610	5.3	597,900	2,6
1976	19,506	7.7	1,250,000	5.4
1979	26,556	9.8	1,140,000	4.3
1982	52,420	19.4	2,626,000	9.9
1985	55,610	22.7	3,113,000	11.3
1987 (Q1)	51,449	20.8	3,078,000	10.9

worldwide overcapacity in iron and steel, partly the result of new capacity in the Newly Industrialising Countries (NICs) such as Brazil, which forced a reduction in the demand for crude steel output while simultaneously the Corporation introduced a drastic programme of rationalisation precisely in order to raise efficiency to cope with the competition from the NICs. Employment in BSC fell from 23,000 to 7,000 over the period 1976—86, a trauma which has been repeated throughout the steel industries of Europe and North America, despite different patterns of ownership and differences in the ostensible ideology of governments. The contraction in investment in the major manufacturing concerns fed through into a collapse in employment in heavy construction, while burgeoning unemployment contributed to a fall of almost one-half in new housing construction. Demand-led services such as retailing suffered in consequence and publicly financed services bore the results of public expenditure restraints.

The explosion in unemployment could fairly be blamed on a number of factors. The drastic loss in British industries' competitiveness was a result of the collapse of the previous Labour Government's incomes policy and the acquiescence of the incoming Conservative administration to the drastic over-valuation of the pound, a stance to be blamed more on naivety and ignorance than on mendacity. Cleveland suffered especially because of its dangerous over-reliance on a narrow range of industries which, like steel, suffered most from shifts in world demand

and from the traditional weaknesses of the British economy which we identified in the last chapter, such as poor industrial relations and inadequate training. It is salutary to note that Cleveland remains overdependent still on too narrow an industrial base.[6]

It would also have to be admitted that some of the seeds of Cleveland's problems lay in the very regional policies which had apparently delivered that period of prosperity in the 1960s and early 1970s, for in this period the vast bulk of employment growth was in the branch plants of major corporations whose headquarters were located elsewhere.[7] In 1976, only 9 per cent of manufacturing jobs were in firms controlled from within the county. Eighty per cent of the workforce was employed in London-based establishments, including of course state-owned BSC and private ICI. In the recession these branch plants have been especially prone to closure and rationalisation and have performed significantly worse in employment terms than smaller, locally-owned establishments.[8] Moreover, closure or job-shedding by corporate 'remote control' increases the sense of powerlessness of the people in Cleveland over their own future, already seemingly dominated by world trends in technology, trade, and all of the forces which cannot be influenced locally.

However, the problems of a regional policy based on the attraction of branch plants extend further. The plants tended to develop few local linkages, purchasing raw materials and components from outside the county, while exporting semi-finished steel and bulk chemicals elsewhere for completion into final products. The branch plants generated short-term jobs in heavy construction, but over three-quarters of the specialised business services purchased by Cleveland-based branch plants come from outside the county. This leads to the more general point that these imported establishments did little to diversify the technical, managerial and skill base of the local economy, being instead largely an extension of existing manual skills. Meanwhile the highly skilled, highly paid (and faster growing) white-collar jobs have continued to be located elsewhere.[9]

The very dependence of Cleveland on large manufacturing plants appears to have had perverse consequences in significantly depressing the growth of indigenous new firms.[10] In 1976, almost three-quarters of manufacturing employment was in large plants employing over five hundred workers. The rate of new firm formation in the county is significantly below the national average, as is the proportion of employment in small firms and the proportion of the labour force in self-employment. The whole problem of Cleveland's reputation for lack of enterprise is investigated further in Chapter 9.

There is considerable controversy over the cost-effectiveness of traditional regional policy, especially because of the very large element of *deadweight* spending. This refers to the use of Regional Development Grants by employers such as ICI and BSC to finance investment which would have taken place without any subsidy. There is also the worry that this heavy investment in capital-intensive manufacturing helped reduce employment by encouraging the big companies to shed labour using the very subsidies whose expressed main purpose was to improve employment.[11] In fact, the whole issue of the costs and benefits of traditional regional policy is something of an academic minefield. Between 1960 and 1981, it is estimated that regional policy may have created over three-quarters of a million jobs in the assisted areas at a gross cost per job of £35,000 at 1984 prices, and most of these jobs were still in existence in 1981. However, it is unclear how many of these jobs were entirely new and how many were at the expense of jobs lost in the non-assisted areas such as the South-East and the West Midlands, and it is also unclear just what the true net costs of these policies have been.[12]

However appropriate were the instruments of large investment subsidies and controls on industrial expansion in the South-East and the West Midlands during the 1960s, they seem far less relevant in the 1980s. The controls are ineffective and indeed perverse, given the absolute national shortage of jobs, while there is certainly no need to pay automatic investment grants to encourage firms to become more capital intensive, for they appear quite happy to do this anyway. To subsidise ICI's operations in Cleveland after the firm has declared over one billion pounds in profits in 1986 would not strike most people as appropriate. To secure a competitive and profitable manufacturing industry would seem to require investment in improving industrial relations and education and training and maintaining a realistic exchange rate, rather than in an industrial and regional policy of the 1960s variety.

By concentrating on branch plants and basic manufacturing, regional policy has failed to attract to Cleveland the high-order business services such as marketing, the research and development establishments, and the corporate headquarters which appear to have provided other areas with a strong base to weather the recession, and has contributed to the concentration of decision making in the greater South-East. In this sense regional policy has been imperfectly targeted at some of the wrong kinds of jobs, neglecting the type of employment which would allow a local economy to begin to generate new prosperity from within itself. Cleveland has a weak managerial base and what skilled management it has is tied to the two big employers. There are no independent financial institutions in the county and Teesside even lacks its own building society. 'Ordinary people travel on trains and roads, economists travel on infrastructure.' So jokes the Prime Minister (or rather her speech writers). The renewal of the infrastructure plays a major role in the employment strategies offered as an alternative to the policies followed since 1979. A focus upon the obsolescence of much of the infrastructure in Cleveland, and proposals for public investment to spearhead improvements in communications, water supply, the provision of serviced industrial land from presently derelict sites, and so on, is one of the centrepieces of programmes which have been proposed for fostering a resurgence of the local economy. Indeed, some of the government's own research accepts much of the case for increased public-sector investment, and we shall see in Chapter 6 that the Urban Development Corporation, answerable directly to London, is to be the main chosen instrument for the direction of this investment.[13]

In Chapter 1 we outlined a set of criteria for trying to judge the merits of policies intended to reduce unemployment; it will be useful now to look at the infrastructure question on the basis of these criteria, taking road building as an example. It must be admitted, first, that building roads is not actually a very cost-effective way of creating employment because it is so capital-intensive. Indeed, the best estimates of the job-creating potential of major road-building schemes suggest that they yield less than one-quarter as many jobs as other forms of public expenditure.[14] Nevertheless, transport improvements could be justified if one could show that they brought major benefits to an economy like Cleveland's by lowering the costs of businesses in the area and improving accessibility to the rest of the country. Unfortunately there is a great scarcity of information on the relationship between transport and other forms of infrastructure spending and regional economic development, and the only major piece of research in this area had to be abandoned for lack of hard facts and good data.[15] Road building demands a variety of high-level skills and it is not obvious that this kind of employment would be suitable for people who have been out of work for a long time. Transport improvements take time to plan and to assemble the necessary land and so on, and thus do not satisfy the fourth of our criteria.

What we can conclude is that the case which has been made for increased infrastructure investment in, for example, transport, remains at best unproven. We can also ram home a more general point and that is just how ignorant we are of the most effective ways of helping the regions of high unemployment and indeed of what makes them unattractive in the first place. It has to be said that the government from 1979 onwards has been as lacklustre as previous administrations in investing time and resources in trying to find out the answers to these questions.

So far we have tried to suggest some reasons why the economy of Cleveland proved so vulnerable to the great employment shock of 1979-81. We have suggested that many of the underlying weaknesses of the county's economy stemmed precisely from the poorly targeted regional policies of the 1960s and 1970s and we have expressed some scepticism about the case for increased infrastructure spending. In fact, in Chapter 11 we hope to put forward the thesis that 'small is beautiful' when it comes to public investment, and that it is wise to be careful about more grandiose projects.

In the next chapter we will try to explain why Cleveland has not been one of the greatest beneficiaries of the modest recovery in employment which has taken place since 1983. We also want to look in more detail at one of the key questions posed in this book: why the long-term unemployed are being by-passed by the unbalanced recovery.

Notes

1. This quote comes from the study by Foord *et al.* (1985), which provides an excellent source of material on the changes on Teesside over two decades.
2. The confusion over what is Teesside and what is Cleveland stems from the botched local government reforms of 1974.
3. The book by North (1979) provides an economic history of Teesside.
4. This is a very important point, for it suggests a sceptical attitude towards the argument that restoration of full employment would be 'a piece of cake', as it allegedly was in the late 1930s. Rearmament in fact ran into massive problems and from 1941 was financed only through American charity (see Barnett 1986).
5. Left-wing critics who bemoan lack of investment by private capital should think carefully about this point.
6. This is stressed in the Department of Trade and Industry submission referred to in note 13 below.
7. The source of much of this chapter lies in work conducted at the Centre for Urban and Regional Development Studies at Newcastle University and some of the work referred to is listed below.
8. See Storey (1985).
9. This argument is developed in Storey (1983).

10. See Fothergill and Gudgin (1982), Storey (1981) and Regional Studies Association (1983).
11. See Robinson and Storey (1981).
12. Armstrong and Taylor (1986) contains an excellent discussion of these issues (and is more favourable to regional policy than we have been). Armstrong and Taylor (1985) is an excellent standard text for regional policy.
13. In 1986 the Department of Trade and Industry made a submission to the European Community emphasising the underdeveloped nature of much of Britain's regional infrastructure. It was, however, a sales pitch to get more money out of Brussels and ought perhaps to be seen in this light.
14. Davies and Metcalf (1985) report that road-building costs £36,000 per unemployed person removed from the register. The House of Commons Parliamentary Unit at the University of Warwick estimates that public current expenditure has a net cost per job of only £8,500. These estimates are both at 1986 prices.
15. The research referred to is Diamond *et al.* (1984). Hausner (1986) is especially critical of the lack of attention to good research in the area of urban and regional economic problems.

3

The Unbalanced Recovery

'In the early 1980s this country went to war to defeat inflation, for the benefit of all. But now the survivors seem to have forgotten the dead and wounded.'[1]

To a certain degree there is not much point in pursuing further the question of precisely who is to blame for the collapse in employment in Britain, 1979—1983. Not that it isn't very useful to have some idea of the causes, if only to make sure that such a trauma is never again repeated. However, pessimists might note that similar remarks were made about the lessons of the Great Depression of the inter-war years, indicating the strange tendency of mankind to learn nothing from history and go on repeating the same errors. Nevertheless, what is done is done, and this chapter proposes instead to investigate the recovery in employment which *has* taken place since the recession came to an end.

It is a familiar boast that since 1983 over one million jobs have been created in the British economy. Given that nearly two million jobs were lost between 1979 and 1983, the cynic might argue that we are half way towards repairing the damage of those four years. Nevertheless, it is worth examining in some detail the growth in the employed labour force of some 1,040,000 between March 1983 and September 1986, and how the recovery might continue to develop in the rest of the decade.[2] Not being cynical myself, I will not stress that this growth in employment is the result precisely of an unannounced U-turn in economic policy in 1983; since then both fiscal and monetary policy have been fairly relaxed and in particular the damagingly high exchange rate of 1979—81 has been reversed.

The figure of employment growth of over one million is composed of an increase in self-employment of some 445,000 and an increase in regular employment of 593,000. This latter figure disguises a growth in service employment of over 1.1 million combined with the loss of a further third of a million jobs in manufacturing and nearly 170,000 jobs in other sectors (such as mining). Over half of the increase in employment (more than 550,000) has been in part-time jobs and substantially over half has gone to females. Finally, there has been an increase of some 300,000 in the number of people with more than one job, and this would seem to account for a lot of the growth in part-time employment.

The best source of information about future employment trends comes from an employer-based survey of over three thousand firms, and a detailed follow-up of a cross section of over four hundred diverse companies carried out by the Institute of Manpower Studies.[3] What is most interesting is the composition of future employment growth as seen by these firms, with up to half of Britain's new jobs going to females, one-quarter likely to be part-time and one in ten in self-employment. One-fifth of the new jobs will go to school leavers. To a large extent, then, this is simply a continuation of the trend which has been dominant since 1983 in that most of the new jobs are going to labour market entrants — women and school leavers — rather than to the long-term unemployed. This explains the crucial paradox that since 1983 one million new jobs have been created, but until 1987 unemployment remained stubbornly above three million. Increased employment of married women, in mainly part-time jobs, does not reduce the official unemployment total because married women are not eligible for benefit and are therefore excluded from the official count which is a measure of those who are out of work and claiming benefit.

We are now in danger of running into the problem of 'lies, damned lies and statistics'. Since 1979 there have been nineteen changes in the definition of what counts as official unemployment.[4] Rather than get bogged down in this 'statistical Stalingrad' we will only emphasise the importance of comparing over time a series of figures which are calculated on the same basis. In February 1987, the official number for those out of work was 3,074,000, and in May 1979, using the *same* method of calculating unemployment, there were 1,153,000 people without a job. We can therefore still emphasise that national unemployment has risen by nearly two million since 1979, or has nearly trebled.[5]

The purpose of this chapter is to emphasise two very important points about the recovery since 1983. Firstly, as we have already described, most of the new jobs have gone to labour market entrants. However, the number of those out of work for more than one year — the long-

Table 3.1 The Growth in Long-Term Unemployment

	1979	1980	1981	1982	1983	1984	1985	1986	1987 (Q1)
Long-term unemployed (000s)	346.8	354.1	515.9	994.4	1,143.4	1,218.2	1,334.2	1,356.5	1,314.8
Long-term as % of all unemployed	23.9	23.3	20.4	33.1	36.5	39.2	40.8	40.8	41.4

term unemployed — has continued to rise so that, by 1986, over 1.3 million people were in this position (Table 3.1): the unbalanced recovery has by-passed the long-term unemployed. Secondly, it is not true that every place in the country has benefited from the recovery. There are many communities which have become unemployment black spots, largely untouched by the growth in job prospects and material affluence from which the rest of use have benefited. This is the other half of what we mean by the unbalanced recovery.

The reader should note that the choice of the word 'community' in the last paragraph was carefully arrived at. Others might have chosen the word 'region' and emphasised the argument that the real imbalance is between the North and the South of Britain — the North–South Gap. Like most clichés, this one has a very strong grain of truth in it, for there has been a difference in the economic fortunes of local areas depending on which side of a line from the Severn to the Wash they happen to lie. Nevertheless, to emphasise the existence of this gap is to insist on a half-truth and to disguise the fact that there are also pockets of severe unemployment in the south of England.

In fact, if we look at the most serious unemployment black spots in the country (Figure 3.1) we arrive at a somewhat more complicated pattern than would be suggested by a simple North–South interpretation. It is true that the long-standing problem areas of the North-East of England, South Yorkshire, Merseyside, Central Scotland and South Wales stand out, as do those more rural areas in the west of the country such as Cornwall, Anglesey and the Western Isles of Scotland which suffer from their isolated position. We can also identify the West Midlands and Teesside with their serious concentrations of high unemployment, a function of their recent and rapid decline from growth zones to black spots. Nevertheless, it is also true that there are communities in the south of England which suffer unemployment rates which are as bad as those in the north, including many wards in inner London and settlements which suffer from specific problems such as Corby in Northants or the Medway towns.

The impression given by Figure 3.1 is that the county of Cleveland is just one big black spot (literally). However, this is misleading, and Figure 3.2 shows the dispersion in unemployment across the county. If we look at the major towns in Cleveland, with which its inhabitants would be familiar (Table 3.2), the male unemployment rate can be seen to vary from under 8 per cent to nearly 50 per cent! The worst unemployment is concentrated along the banks of the River Tees, in North-Central

Figure 3.1 The 10% of Wards with the Highest Unemployment
Rates, 1981

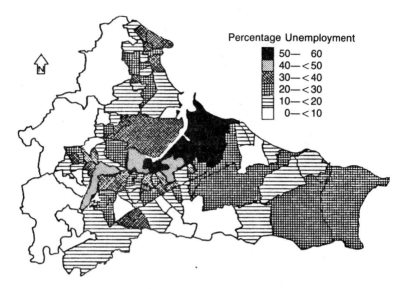

Percentage Unemployment

50— 60
40—<50
30—<40
20—<30
10—<20
0—<10

Figure 3.2 Male Unemployment in Cleveland (By District
Electoral Wards, April 1986)

Middlesbrough, South Bank and Grangetown. These are the communities
worst hit by closures in steel, heavy engineering and shipbuilding: they
form a string of wards where about half of the men are out of work.
Nevertheless, there are also two types of community where unemployment is at or below the national average — small market towns such
as Yarm and the pleasant communities on the fringe of the Teesside conurbation such as Guisborough, Marske and South Middlesbrough, where
the county's good housing and its professional and managerial classes
are concentrated. If we look further afield we are struck by the similarities
between Yarm and the market towns of North Yorkshire such as
Pickering, Harrogate and Ripon, all of which boast unemployment rates
substantially below the national average.

If we look at the pattern of very hard-hit communities and compare
them with the more prosperous labour markets in the country as a whole,
four important points emerge.[6] The first is the *North—South Gap*, for
it is true that the most prosperous communities all lie in the belt running
from Cambridge to Milton Keynes and on to the M4 corridor from
Newbury to West London and south into Hampshire and Surrey. Nevertheless it is also true that these successful towns are of small or
intermediate size, indeed almost semi-rural in character. The regional

Table 3.2 Unemployment in the Main Towns of
Cleveland (%)

Major settlements in Cleveland	Unemployment rate (May 1986)		
	Male	Female	Total
Billingham	21.2	15.4	18.9
Eaglescliffe	8.9	9.1	9.0
Guisborough	13.3	11.1	12.5
Hartlepool	25.4	15.5	21.7
Marske/New Marske	11.6	9.8	10.9
Middlesbrough	28.9	14.8	23.6
Redcar	24.4	16.2	21.3
South Bank	49.7	28.1	43.4
Stockton	25.0	14.9	21.2
Thornaby	26.5	15.7	22.4
Yarm	7.5	9.0	8.1

pattern is thus overlaid by an *urban–rural* divide which explains the existence of prospering towns in the north such as Harrogate. In addition we have the contrast between the *inner city* and the more prosperous outer suburbs which is true for every region. Thus we can compare the centre of the Teesside conurbation with South Middlesbrough, or the Manchester conurbation with Macclesfield, or Tower Hamlets with Harrow, and so on.[7] Finally, there is *industrial structure,* which is heavily negative for towns dependent on a very narrow manufacturing base (such as Corby or Consett) and strongly positive for towns with an above-average concentration of financial and business services (for example Winchester). However, the influence of manufacturing as a whole should not perhaps be exaggerated. Cleveland and the West Midlands are unusual in that their heavy dependence on certain sectors of manufacturing is an important reason for their poor performance. Cleveland has lost nearly half of its manufacturing jobs compared with just over a quarter of manufacturing jobs in the country as a whole. The East Midlands has not suffered so greatly, despite its overdependence on a disadvantaged manufacturing sector (in this case clothing).[8]

Britain's provincial boom towns share certain things in common, tending to be smaller service centres for larger rural areas, without a strong manufacturing tradition but close enough to a major conurbation to benefit from the presence of commuters.[9] However, to talk about an urban–rural, or indeed a North–South, shift in employment may give the impression that there are large numbers of firms on the move to new locations. This is misleading, for the actual migration of firms accounts for only a relatively small proportion of employment change. In the disadvantaged inner cities, the northern conurbations and the single-industry towns, we have a process of plant closures and rationalisations. Meanwhile it is in the small and medium-sized towns that new firms are setting up and existing ones are expanding, especially if these towns are located in the south. The question is, what makes a particular place attractive to a new or expanding firm?

The first thing to realise is that most firms feel that they do not have the time or the need to choose a location on rigorously objective grounds. Only 25 per cent of firms actually carry out a serious relocation study, the rest rely on intuition (or prejudice) and the majority perception is that the south of England offers precisely the patterns of settlement, the quality of environment, of schools and so on, which fit in with the preferences of key sections of the workforce and management.[10] The north is perceived as having major problems with the quality of the labour force and the quality of life, except for those choice, semi-rural locations which we have mentioned earlier.

In addition to this influence of perceived image, the greater south-east has the advantage of London's dominance as the great business, financial, administrative and political centre of the United Kingdom, with its nodal position in the national and international communications networks. The greater south-east claims the lion's share of research and development establishments, both public and private, and benefits from a concentration of qualified manpower. Increasingly, it is no longer so true that people move to where the jobs are available, but rather that the presence of people available for work attracts the firms. This is why personal preferences on where to live are having a growing influence on the location of employment.

The correlation between population change, employment change and unemployment is not exact and the causal interrelationship between these factors is hard to untangle. A growth in population generates employment, both because of the presence of an available labour force and because of the demand for services generated by the increasing number of people. A prosperous labour market will in turn attract further population growth, although the growth in people can sometimes be so rapid that employment struggles to keep pace, as has been the case with Milton Keynes, for example.[11] An even more crucial point to register is that the creation of jobs in a particular locality does *not* necessarily reduce unemployment in that locality. This is especially true for the inner city where any jobs which are generated may go to outsiders who are commuting in, rather than to residents. As we shall see in Chapter 6, to bring employment to the London Docklands may reduce unemployment in Crawley, but leave it untouched in Tower Hamlets.

Are we correct in stressing that the preference of firms and the key members of their workforce for locations in the south or in the semi-rural areas of the north, rather than the conurbations, is based more on prejudice that on rationality? It is true that Teesside lacks major cultural attractions and its leisure facilities are underutilised and tourism underdeveloped. However, good and inexpensive housing in the area is available and can match anything in the south of the country. As we shall see in Chapter 12, Cleveland's education authority is ranked amongst the top ten in the country (along with Manchester, Newcastle and Liverpool) and overall the performance of local education authorities is completely uncorrelated with regional location. The county boasts easy access to some of the most beautiful rural environment in Britain. To suggest that there are problems with the overall quality of the labour force is misleading, as foreign firms locating in the North-East have found out and noted, to their pleasant surprise.

If we were to take a really historical view of things, then the geographical pattern which is being established today is not unlike the pattern of pre-industrial revolution Britain, with prosperity based in the south and in the rural areas. The great rise of the northern manufacturing conurbations was a function of the reliance of the industrial revolution on coal as its energy source. But as coal has lost its place as a crucial factor in determining the spread of economic activity, so are we reverting to a more traditional pattern of location. However, change is a process, not an event, and the Frenchman who coined the term industrial 'revolution' actually did the study of economic and social change a disservice. Neither does change follow a 'natural' or God-given pattern, but is the result of the decisions of individuals. This is especially true when we consider the influence of image on the growth and decline of communities, where it would seem that Orwell's *Road to Wigan Pier* dominates Marshall's *Principles of Economics*.

Long-Term Unemployment

The longer a person is out of work, the less chance he or she has of finding a job. This is the trap into which the long-term unemployed have fallen. Figure 3.3 shows that for those who have been out of work for

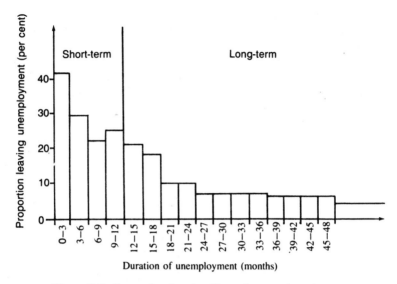

Figure 3.3   Proportion Leaving Unemployment in a Quarter
by Duration (First Quarter 1984)

only a couple of months, there is actually a reasonable chance of leaving unemployment. But the chances of finding a job decline quite quickly as the duration of unemployment lengthens, so that a person who is approaching his second year without work has less than a 10 per cent chance of finding a job in any quarter.

A much greater proportion of older, unemployed men has been out of work for over a year (Figure 3.4). In Cleveland well over two-thirds of those unemployed men over forty-five have been out of work for more than twelve months. We can also see that Cleveland has a much higher proportion of young people in their twenties who have been out of work for a very long time. This is the age group which missed out on the expanding youth training measures which were instituted in the early 1980s or, if it participated in such schemes, many of its members left for unemployment rather than obtaining work. This age group and the older long-term unemployed represent the most intractable core of the unemployment problem, although it is not clear that public perception has caught up with this reality and with the fact that school leaver unemployment is a problem of declining, though still serious, importance.[12]

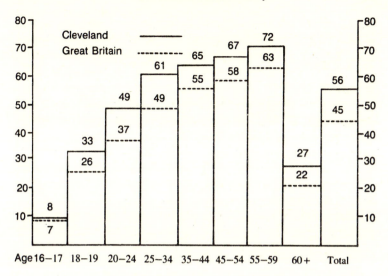

Figure 3.4 Percentage of Unemployed Men Who Are Long-Term Unemployed: Cleveland and Great Britain (July 1986)

When a person who has been out of work for a very long time does find a job, it does not necessarily last. What imperfect information we have suggests that over half of the unemployed men who find work fail to retain their new jobs for any length of time.[13] This phenomenon of recurrent unemployment is especially worrying for young people who are never in jobs long enough to learn any significant skills. For many of the long-term unemployed, the only jobs they can obtain are often part-time, low-paid, involving little use of skills and less training and with little job security, either because of redundancy or because the jobs were explicitly temporary in the first place (in Chapter 7 we will note how the Community Programme organised by the Manpower Services Commission replicates this same pattern of work). In Cleveland, two-thirds of unemployed teenagers and over one-third of the long-term unemployed in their early twenties said that they had no normal kind of work which emphasises our point about lack of job stability among the young.[14]

It has been suggested that those who have been out of work for a long time tend to give up on the search for jobs and this accounts for the fact that they tend to get trapped into very long-term unemployment. Actually, it is remarkable just how long unemployed people continue searching for jobs, even in a labour market like Cleveland's, where the chances of finding work are so poor (Table 3.3). It is only when someone has been out of work for five years or more, or begins to approach his fifties, that intensity of job search seems to fall sharply.[15] A man who has been out of work for five years and is fifty years old can rationally expect that he is highly unlikely to be offered anything, and the decision to stop looking for work so assiduously appears quite sensible. Indeed, those responsible for the administration of the social security system put little pressure on these older long-term unemployed, for the circumstances of the labour market are such that it could not possibly do any good to exert any pressure. However, many of these older long-term unemployed will have records of years of stable employment (perhaps decades even, working for BSC or ICI), so that their present partial withdrawal from the labour market is not indicative of their entire working lives.[16]

Table 3.3   Percentage of Respondents Who had Visited a Job Centre in Cleveland in the Previous Month, by Age and Duration of Unemployment (Spring 1985)

Age	*16−19*	*20−24*	*25−44*	*45−65*	
Per cent	84	80	75	49	

Duration of unemployment (years)		*−1*	*1−3*	*3−5*	*5+*
Per cent		80	73	72	54

It could not be argued that the unemployed in Cleveland are very demanding. A survey of over sixteen hundred unemployed people from some of the county's black spots (of whom over two-thirds had been out of work for more than a year) revealed that nearly four out of five men and over two-thirds of the women were looking for any job going, at skill levels similar to or below their previous work.[17] Nearly all the men and two-thirds of the women preferred full-time work, but 85 per cent of women and over half the men said they would accept part-time jobs. Only just over one in five men and hardly any women expected a minimum take-home pay of over one hundred pounds a week for a full-time job and nearly all women and nearly half the men said they would accept eighty pounds or less. Nine out of ten teenagers said that they would accept a wage of sixty pounds or less and over two-thirds of the unemployed in their early twenties expected less than eighty pounds a week.

The Cleveland survey found that the importance attached to finding a job or the degree of effort put into job search were not associated with the level of benefit income or the size of any redundancy payments from previous employment. Though the social security system does not appear to affect the intensity of job search it could be argued that family men might turn down job offers if they received them because their benefit payments exceeded the low pay on offer. It might be more accurate to say, however, that the family man is unlikely to receive any offers in the first place, and fewer than one in ten of the respondents in Cleveland had ever turned down any job opportunity. Moreover, if one unemployed person turns down a job because of low pay, it is not at all clear that aggregate unemployment is affected, for the job will simply be taken up by a teenager or married woman for whom the low pay is not a deterrent. It is very hard indeed to pin the blame for the rise in unemployment on an over-generous benefits system, for that system has become significantly less generous since 1979, with the abolition of earnings-related unemployment benefit and the taxation of unemployment benefit. Fewer than one in forty of the long-term unemployed receive, through the benefits system, more than 90 per cent of their previous income when in work.[18]

One aspect of Cleveland's labour market which receives considerable attention in the media is the so-called black economy. Since the recession, firms such as BSC have contracted out much of their maintenance work, and so on, to smaller firms, many of whom, it is alleged, use unemployed people working on very short 'contracts' of only a few weeks, paying them cash in hand while the workers continue to claim benefits illegally. In autumn 1986 prosecutions began of over 100 people allegedly engaged in this form of fraud working for BSC sub-contractors.

Firm evidence is very hard to come by and most people's impression of the black economy is gained from often sensationalist newspaper reports based on anecdotes. The most detailed analysis of the black economy at the national level indicates its size as perhaps 3 to 6 per cent of GNP, substantially below what one would expect from an analysis of media reports and popular prejudice, and substantially below the size of the illegal sector in countries such as Italy.[19] Is it possible that Cleveland's informal sector is larger than this? It is highly unlikely — the prosperity of the black economy is dependent on the prosperity of

the formal economy. Only if households have money to spare on repairing their homes, or firms have cash to invest in maintenance programmes, will there be a demand for informal economic activity paid for by
cash. The stunting of Cleveland's formal economy must inhibit the size
of its informal economy.[20]

Even if the black economy were of a significant size, the evidence
is that it is *not* the unemployed who are the main participants. A detailed
study of the labour market in the Isle of Sheppey suggested that most
of the work in the black economy is performed by moonlighters: people
already in jobs who use their employment to gain access to information
about work opportunities for cash in hand and then borrow their
employers' tools to do the job.[21] The unemployed have neither access
to such information nor the tools to participate. Surveys of the
unemployed find that few actually admit to working in the black economy
(only 8 per cent in one survey[22]), but many believe other unemployed
people do participate. Take two unemployed men in a pub: ask Jack and
he will say he is not working and claiming benefit illegally, but that Fred
is; ask Fred and he will claim innocence but will acuse Jack of being
the villain. From such anecdotes grow the misleading claims about the
size of the problem.

Another argument which is frequently heard is that many of Cleveland's
workers (including some who are claiming benefit) are working on short-
term contracts in the south of England, the North Sea or abroad, while
retaining homes and family in Cleveland. There are anecdotes about
southern-based employers busing people from the county to work from
Monday to Friday on construction sites in the south-east and sending
them home at weekends. Again, hard evidence is difficult to come by,
but analysis of population census data indicates that only one or two per
cent of the county's labour force is employed outside of Cleveland, and
this figure is more likely to be declining, given the collapse in oil prices
and the fall in employment opportunities in offshore work. We can also
speculate that participation in this kind of work demands specific skills
and access to informal information networks. On both these counts, the
long-term unemployed are at a disadvantage.

We are as yet no closer to explaining why the long-term unemployed
are significantly less likely than those who have been out of work for
only a short period of time to receive job offers and find work. We have
suggested that the benefits system plays little role and that the unemployed
themselves continue to search quite actively for work unless they are
older and have been without jobs for a very long period of time indeed.

We are left with the thesis that it is employers' reluctance to hire people who have been out of work for a long time which accounts for the latter's low escape probabilities.

A survey of over one thousand employers in the Group of Five leading industrial nations (the United States, Japan, West Germany, France and Britain) revealed that two out of five employers admit that they are reluctant to take on the long-term unemployed.[23] British employers emerged as the most conservative with half of them expecting to make profits by shedding labour. Many employers faced with a large number of applications for a limited number of jobs will use some simple rules of thumb designed to screen out as many applicants as possible at an early stage. Age and duration of unemployment are two of the most important rules. In Chapter 10 we shall review some further disturbing evidence on the attitudes of British employers which strongly suggests that they would not change their recruitment policies and tilt them towards the long-term unemployed even if they were offered a large financial incentive to do so.

The report referred to earlier by the Institute of Manpower Studies also paints a portrait of defensive employers who are happy to recruit people with significant skills (who are often already employed by someone else) or to take on teenagers and married women to fill the low-paid and low-skilled jobs which are available, but who retain deep suspicions about those people who have been out of work for a long time. Here we have the rub. Left-wing commentators sometimes assert that the recession was deliberately engineered by a government determined to 'teach the workers a lesson', to show them who was in charge and to lower expectations about pay and conditions for the lower half of the labour force. Perhaps there is a grain of truth in this. But the real consequence of the recession seems to have been the lesson it has taught employers, and the lesson is one of retrenchment and the sharp cutting of costs to remain competitive. If you are able to increase output, try to do it with your existing core labour force or, if you must recruit, take on labour market entrants, but certainly not people who have been out of work for a long time, for their morale might be low and their skills eroded.

Are employers acting rationally in believing that the long-term unemployed have indeed lost their skills and their morale? As we shall see in the next chapter, it is true that low morale amongst the unemployed is a major problem, but it is a function of the fear that they might never find work again. Offer the long-term unemployed person the chance of a job of reasonable quality, prospects and pay, and morale should take about ten minutes to recover fully. The question mark hanging over the skills of the long-term unemployed is far more difficult to answer. This difficulty stems in part from the lack of good information on the skills of the unemployed. The Restart initiative, which was launched by the Manpower Services Commission in 1986, was not clearly directed to gather useful information on the past experience and training of the long-term unemployed and was only just beginning to ask serious questions in 1987 (see Chapter 7). Nevertheless, what we do know is not encouraging. Those who have been out of work for over two years are only half as likely to have academic qualifications such as 'O' or 'A' levels, and nearly six out of ten report no qualifications whatsoever (Table 3.4). More recent information suggests that of those men aged between twenty-five and fifty-four, who have been out of work for over one year, about two-thirds have no qualifications, and this is to be compared with only 46 per cent of the short-term unemployed and 27 per cent of the employed labour force who are without qualifications. Another worrying indicator is that one in four of the long-term unemployed seem to have significant problems with basic literacy and numeracy, a total of some 350–400,000 individuals.[24] A detailed breakdown of the former occupations of the sixteen hundred unemployed surveyed in Cleveland indicated that the majority of respondents had formerly held semi- or unskilled jobs or had previously worked in industries such as steel or heavy engineering, so that the skills they did have were now probably redundant.[25] It is not therefore simply the case that the skills of the long-term unemployed erode over time, but that they never possessed any significant skills to begin with or possessed skills which are no longer in demand.

Table 3.4 The Qualifications of the Unemployed

Qualifications	*Short-term* *(less than 6 months)*	*Long-term* *(more than 2 years)*
Higher education	8	3
'A' and 'O' level and equivalent	33	17
Apprenticeship	6	8
CSE below grade 1 and other qualifications	13	11
No qualifications	40	58

This is very worrying, for the demand for semi- and unskilled labour is declining, and what demand there is for this kind of labour appears to be drawing mainly on the supply of labour market entrants. The increasing demand for people with professional and managerial skills, engineers, technicians and multiple-skilled craftsmen, appears likely to by-pass the long-term unemployed. Employers seem to presume that the older, long-term unemployed are not likely to prove adaptable to new technologies or working practices and would be unwilling to learn new skills. It was indeed the case in Cleveland that most long-term unemployed people were generally dismissive of the value of further education and training and few were taking advantage of courses in new technology.[26]

It has been argued that the rearmament boom of the late 1930s and the outbreak of the Second World War allowed for a relatively trouble-free assimiliation of the long-term unemployed into the wartime labour force. But of course a war boosts demand for tanks and ships and air-craft and thus helps the recovery of heavy engineering, shipbuilding, steel and coal, precisely the industries from which the unemployed may have come originally, but which are unlikely to see the same recovery in employment today. Moreover, the portrait which is often painted of an efficient and happy domestic economy in Britain from 1940 to 1945 appears to be a myth.[27]

Conclusion

It is time to draw together the two strands of this chapter. The unbalanced economic recovery is by-passing the long-term unemployed and it is also leaving behind whole communities, north and south. These two processes are intimately interrelated, for it is precisely the consequences of living in certain disadvantaged neighbourhoods which can have a significant effect on an individual's chances of being trapped in long-term unemploy-ment.[28] The problem is the concentration within one community of poor local schools and a high proportion of young people leaving school without qualifications; limited access to information networks regarding employment opportunities, especially for those who have been out of work for some time; restricted mobility because of lack of income or poor public transport; and the discrimination of employers against people from certain perceived 'problem areas'. We can perhaps link together the problems of people being left out of the recovery because they live in the wrong neighbourhood, have been ill-served by the education system, are too old, have been out of work for too long, or have the incorrect skin colour. What can be said is that the economic recovery is not 'trickling down' to the most disadvantaged communities, suggesting the need for not just a somewhat faster pace of recovery but a fundamentally more balanced share-out of the benefits of economic prosperity.[29]

Notes

1. The words of a former senior Treasury official quoted in *The Financial Times,* March 27, 1987.
2. The figures quoted in this and the following paragraph come from the 1986 Labour Force Survey.
3. For the Occupational Studies Group, published as Rajan and Pearson (1986)
4. For those who have the stamina, the best guide to these issues are the various briefings available from the Unemployment Unit, especially Issue 22, Winter 1986, page 14.
5. This consistent series was worked out by economists in the Department of Employment.
6. Much of the analysis in this first half of Chapter 3 draws on work by the Centre for Urban and Regional Development Studies (CURDS) at Newcastle University, brought together in Champion *et al.* (1987).
7. Actually, the pattern in London is even more complicated than suggested here. See Buck *et al.* (1986) for a more complete analysis.
8. Fothergill and Gudgin (1982) directly compare Cleveland and the East Midlands, making the point that the East Midlands has performed better, despite also having an industrial structure which might be considered disadvantaged.
9. This point is made in Champion *et al.* (1987). See also Townsend (1986), who notes the suprisingly wide dispersion in employment growth, 1978–81.
10. The reference here is to a survey commissioned by the Department of the Environment from the Industrial Building Bureau, *Accommodation Needs of Modern Industry,* published in May 1987. Keeble (1976) was the first social scientist to draw attention to the importance of image in determining locational decisions.
11. See Champion *et al.* (1987).
12. See Chapter 12 for further discussion, and also Rajan and Pearson (1986).
13. See Stern (1986) and White (1983).
14. See Begley (1986).
15. Obviously, visiting a job centre is only one of a number of methods of job search. More informal job information networks are especially important in Cleveland. A visit to a job centre does not necessarily indicate active job search. Nevertheless, we have to work with what evidence we have.

16. The same point is made in White (1983).
17. This is the Cleveland County Council survey *Cleveland's Unemployed, A Summary Report* (1986a), and other council reports listed in the bibliography.
18. See Atkinson and Micklewright (1986) for the most extensive survey of the evidence available on the effects of the benefits system on unemployment. See also Dilnot and Morris (1983) for estimates of the replacement ratios of the long-term unemployed.
19. See Smith (1986).
20. I owe this point (along with many others) to Fred Robinson at CURDS.
21. The excellent study by Ray Pahl (1984).
22. Economist Intelligence Unit (1982).
23. See the special report in *The Financial Times,* 'Work: The Way Ahead', 24 July 1986.
24. These results are from the 1986 Labour Force Survey.
25. See Begley (1986).
26. See Note 17.
27. See Barnett (1986).
28. This argument is strongly developed in an unpublished paper from CURDS by A. Green and D. Owen on 'Long-Term Unemployment'.
29. This is strongly argued in Hausner (1986) and was the punch-line in a report by the Director General of NEDO, delivered to the National Economic Development Council in February 1987.

4
The Consequences of Long-Term Unemployment

'When an individual is no longer a true participant, when he no longer feels a sense of responsibility to his society, the content of democracy is emptied.'[1]

It is a very strange thing that economists are never really expected to think hard about what unemployment means to the individual. In fact, the effects of unemployment on individuals and the communities in which they live are not well researched at all, despite the efforts of other social scientists to try to compensate for the lack of interest shown by economists. In Cleveland, in 1986, over 50,000 people were without work and over half of these had been out of work for more than one year. 13,000 have been out of work for over three years, over 5,000 for more than five years (including, incredibly, over 500 aged under twenty-five). However, these are statistics and it is quite easy to rattle off statistics without ever really thinking about what they mean.

Fortunately, another of the virtues of the survey of unemployed people in Cleveland which we used in the last chapter is that it gives us some guide to how people without work think that their unemployment affects them. We can use this evidence along with the results of other work to try to paint a portrait of the consequences of unemployment for individuals, their families, and the wider community.

People in work don't realise the problems we have, they think it's our fault we are out of work.[2]

Even in an area like Cleveland, where unemployment is so high, there is still a stigma of sorts attached to being jobless. This must reflect the fact that an individual's job is often regarded as the basis of his social status. When asked what one does, it is hard to admit '. . . well, nothing, I'm unemployed'. Even the unemployed themselves will often admit to having looked down upon those out of work before they themselves lost their jobs. The gradual erosion of self-esteem, partly a function of the low opinion often held by the employed of the unemployed, is the first consequence of not having a job, and this erosion appears to be greater the longer an individual is without work.

It is sometimes argued that those without work should be grateful for the extra leisure time they are being awarded — argued, that is, by those *with* jobs who look forward to their holiday periods. However, a fortnight's break from a regular job is pleasant precisely because it is of limited duration, with the prospect of a return to work. But for those out of work for long periods, the time stretches into interminable boredom. It would appear that the period of unemployment which could be regarded as a holiday lasts only a few weeks before the sheer tedium of having nothing to do begins to make its impact. For those who have never experienced unemployment it is useful to think back to childhood and the immense difficulty of filling in the six weeks of the summer holidays, especially as boredom grows towards the end of August. Then consider the results of six months or six years of inactivity. Human beings need activity and need to feel useful — it is a part of our make-up.

There is considerable evidence that the unemployed tend to under-utilise social facilities such as leisure centres, swimming pools, and so on. This is partly a consequence of being unable to afford entrance charges or the transport costs necessary to visit leisure facilities, which are often badly located away from the dour housing estates which are unemployment black spots. Nevertheless, it is also true that *free* facilities such as libraries are also under-utilised by people who are out of work. In Cleveland only 5 per cent of the unemployed sampled were currently involved in any form of voluntary work. Few of the unemployed had undergone any further education or training since losing their jobs, and only 2 per cent had taken a course relating to a leisure interest. More than two-thirds admitted to being very bored most of the time. This tends to reinforce the results of other studies which report an enormous degree of apathy amongst those without work: the tendency is to stay at home and watch the TV 'soaps'.[3]

Before the reader starts moralising, it is worth noting that those Conservative MPs who have bravely tried to spend *one whole week* on supplementary benefit in order to prove that unemployment is not so bad, report that most of their time seemed to be spent in front of the TV.

It would seem to be the case then that work and leisure are complementary — people require a mixture of both. Endless, enforced leisure is a grinding experience.

The MPs referred to above were attempting to prove that the supplementary benefit payments available to the unemployed constituted an adequate income — that no-one without work was in 'poverty'. This is a minefield of semantics, for no-one has ever satisfactorily defined just what constitutes being poor. Clearly everyone would regard starvation in Africa as absolute poverty and no-one would argue that anyone in Britain faces the same fate. In arguing that there are poor people in Britain, all we are saying is that there are individuals and families who have an unacceptably low standard of living relative to what the rest of us have grown used to in the affluent society. To argue that we should not worry about the elderly person who cannot heat her home properly, or the unemployed person who cannot buy his children birthday presents, because they are better off than if they were living in Ethiopia or in this country a hundred years ago, is fatuous. To judge whether or not people should be considered poor we have to make reference to the standards that the majority are used to in Britain in the 1980s.

> Married with three children, three years unemployed. Savings vanish very quickly. Each Christmas becomes more difficult as the children grow. They cannot have the same privileges, holidays, school trips, etc. as their fellow school kids from employed families.[4]

> I feel worse because I can't provide for them. Go without clothes, pocket money, presents — things you would buy for them.[5]

The supplementarry benefits system, on which two out of three of the unemployed rely, was designed as a safety net to catch those few people not covered by insurance benefits. Unemployment benefit only lasts one year because the architect of post-war social security, William Beveridge, did not believe that governments would ever be so stupid as to return to the situation of the 1930s, with many hundreds of thousands of individuals out of work for so long. Supplementary benefit was never meant to cope with providing long-term incomes to the eight million people now dependent on it. These incomes are not generous: a family with two children aged five and ten receives a basic £68.05 per week.[6]

It is often remarked that in Cleveland many of the unemployed are able to rely on substantial redundancy payments from the big firms like ICI and BSC. In the sample we are using, less than two out of five reported receiving any lump sum payment in the last five years and this fits in well with national evidence which suggests that only 4 per cent of those made redundant in the recession received over £5,000, while over one-third received nothing.[7] The 'golden handshake' appears to be very much the exception, not the rule, and is another myth to nail. Moreover, even generous redundancy payments do not postpone financial hardship for very long, not least because anyone with over £3,000 in savings is not allowed to claim supplementary benefit, so there is an incentive built into the system to run savings down below this level. Some two-thirds of the unemployed surveyed in Cleveland had no significant savings.

The ungenerous nature of the supplementary benefits system takes time to bite, for the benefits available to the unemployed are expressly designed for short-term contingencies only. It is when it is time to replace worn-out clothes, furniture and so on, for which the basic rates do not specifically cater, that hardship can begin. One study of families with children in receipt of supplementary benefit found that half ran out of money most weeks, 60 per cent lacked a complete standard set of clothing, and over half were in debt when interviewed.[8] Another study asked a sample of people from all walks of life what *they* (not the sociologists) thought was a decent standard of living to which everyone in Britain today should be entitled.[9] As a consequence of unemployment, over one and a half million adults and nearly one million children were below this standard, as defined by the general public, and three quarters of a million adults and half a million children were unable to afford a whole range of things considered necessities by the rest of society.

> People just get in their flats and don't mix. They just lock their doors and stay in.[10]

In the Cleveland survey, three-quarters of the unemployed said that half or more of their friends were unemployed, and a very sad 5 per cent said that they had no friends. The unemployed tend not to venture out too often, perhaps because they fear the patronising attitudes they might encounter from those people who are in work. Indeed, the workplace is often the source of many friends but these contacts can erode after a lengthy period of unemployment. Most unemployed people, being human, are quite proud and therefore feel enormously uncomfortable when a friend who is in work offers simply to buy them a drink, and this contributes to the process of isolation which can develop.

We shout and argue more. Get on each other's nerves. In the house too much during the day. Get under each other's teet.[11]

I have had more arguments in the family in the first month of being unemployed than in all my sixteen years ...[12]

Nearly one-half of those unemployed people who were married felt that their relationship with their spouse had deteriorated since unemployment began. Only 5 per cent reported an improvement. The effect of unemployment on the relationship between parents and their children is not clear. An equal number felt that relations had improved, because the parent now had more time to spend with his/her children, as felt that relations had worsened. However, other national evidence claims that child abuse is more prevalent in the families of the unemployed.[13]

It would appear to be the case that, when an unemployed person has the help of a supportive extended family and lives in a fairly cohesive and self-contained community, this can have a significant bearing on their ability to cope with and adjust to the problems of being out of work. This may confirm two old adages: that a trouble shared is a trouble halved, and that there are virtues to living in the close-knit 'northern community' so beloved in English literature. The Cleveland Survey showed that psychological wellbeing differed significantly between the four communities which were looked at. The more long-standing communities showed fewer signs of stress than the newer, more anonymous estates close to town centres. Nevertheless, in the sample as a whole, about half of those out of work showed significant psychological distress, as measured by the General Health Questionnaire.[14] The unemployed are more than twice as likely to show signs of psychological stress as the employed and this increases with age, with the time spent out of work, and for those who previously had skilled jobs.

The effects of unemployment on health constitute yet another minefield. The most recent and comprehensive survey of the evidence on this issue confirms the results presented in the previous paragraph, that unemployment can cause a significant deterioration in mental health.[15] Among a group of school leavers who had similar scores on the General Health Questionnaire while at school, it was found that those who left to find jobs showed significantly fewer signs of psychological problems than those who left for unemployment.[16] However, the evidence on a link between unemployment and physical, as opposed to mental, ill health is somewhat less conclusive. This is not surprising because it is extremely hard to disentangle the precise causes of physical ill health, of which unemployment is only one of many. It is unclear whether the unemployed become unhealthy or the unhealthy become unemployed. Nevertheless, one careful study which followed for ten years men who were seeking work in 1971 found that their death rates were 21 per cent higher than normal, even allowing for the fact that unemployment is concentrated amongst the unskilled who tend to have more health problems anyway.[17] Moreover, mortality rates among their wives were also 20 per cent higher than among other married women. Even more disturbingly, other studies indicate that the height of children with an unemployed father, even allowing for differences in social class, is significantly less than the height of children whose fathers are in work.[18] These two pieces of evidence suggest a real effect of unemployment on the health of the families of the unemployed. The leading cause of death amongst the wives of the unemployed was a heart condition related to stress and this ties in with the evidence on the psychological problems created by unemployment, the boredom, the isolation, the worry over finances and the effects on the rest of the family of prolonged joblessness.

If the possible link between unemployment and physical ill health is something of a minefield, the argument over a link between unemployment and crime is like a full-scale battlefield. Unemployment statistics may be unreliable, but crime statistics are a lot worse. There has been as yet only one very careful study which followed over four hundred working-class males from the age of eight or nine through a period of leaving school at the ages of fourteen, sixteen and eighteen.[19] Unemployed youths who were already disadvantaged by coming from large, low-income families in bad housing with relatively neglectful parents and a low achievement at school were significantly more likely to commit non-violent offences for financial gain (such as theft). However, there was no link between unemployment and more serious crimes including rape, assault or drug offences (and also vandalism) and young people with more stable backgrounds were *not* more likely to commit a crime because of unemployment.

> What can anyone do about it? When I think of all the work that needs doing
> . . . and yet there are so many brickies and builders out of work. But what
> can you do about it, you could sit here and talk about it until next July. There
> is nothing you can do about it. We can't create jobs, can we?[20]

If there is one thing that comes across most strongly about unemployed people it is the sense of helplessness, resignation and fatalism. In

Cleveland nearly half of the unemployed did not expect to find work within a year. Over half of those unemployed for more than three years did not expect to find a job at all in the near future. It seems to puzzle many people that prolonged joblessness does not lead to more significant trouble, but the dominant reaction to unemployment is disillusionment, not disorder, and resignation, not riot.

The first thing to stress is that the unemployed are a minority and to an extent an isolated minority. This is particularly true in a great city like London where it is possible to commute from the home counties to an office in Whitehall or the City, by-passing entirely the problems of Brixton or Tower Hamlets which are buried beneath the veneer of an affluent society. Since the end of the recession in 1982, those in work no longer feel the threat of rising unemployment and have had the benefit of steadily increasing wages which, for most people, have outpaced prices and have been reinforced by cuts in taxation. Moreover, although opinion polls report unemployment as the most important issue facing the country as a whole, they also report that fear of inflation remains a major concern to the individual and his or her family.[21]

The second point to stress is fatalism and the absence of willingness to lay blame. For very many people, both in work and out of work, high unemployment is seen as the inevitable consequence of 'technology' or trends in the world economy. In 1982 only one quarter of the unemployed themselves laid the chief blame for their situation on Mrs Thatcher's Government, while nearly half blamed 'nobody' or 'the world economic situation'.[22] Moreover, there is a very deep cynicism about the ability of any other political party to reverse the situation and reach the levels of low unemployment sustained in the first thirty years of the post-war period and which are still sustained in Japan, Sweden and some other countries. The extent to which the 'experts' bicker amongst themselves over the causes of unemployment and the best ways to bring it down can only reinforce the all-pervading sense of resignation. It is a combination of fatalism amongst the unemployed and a creeping complacency amongst the employed which is most worrying.

What can you do about it anyway? Suppose you, the reader, and I, the author, agreed wholeheartedly about the causes of and cures for unemployment, what could we do then? As the individual wisely argued in the quote above, we can't create jobs, can we? Real poverty amongst unemployed families is not just about lack of income, or bad housing and ill health, but about not being able to change anything, not having any influence over events, not having a voice in the decisions which affect their lives — a kind of 'political' poverty, I suppose.[23] For the long-term unemployed have been by-passed by our political processes just as surely as they have been by-passed by the unbalanced recovery. This is the key point being emphasised by Martin Luther King in the passage with which we began this chapter. He was referring directly to the disadvantages of skin colour, but at the back of his mind he always realised the links that exist between the powerlessness of all of those excluded from our democracy because of their race, their ill health, their poverty, their disability or their joblessness.

Any programme to tackle unemployment must recognise that people have a right to 'own' their own problems and to contribute to the construction of solutions for their problems. In Chapter 11 we hope to illustrate how this principle can actually be put into practice. In the meantime it is important to consider the following two questions: are feelings like helplessness, frustration, fatalism, cynicism and resignation really going to contribute to the fundamental resurgence in enterprise and the willingness to accept risk which is at the heart of the new economic policy? And can we really sustain a tolerant and healthy democracy in the long run when so many of our fellow citizens feel that they are no part of it and that the system does not give a damn?

Notes

1. Martin Luther King, Jr.
2. A 54-year-old unemployed person in Cleveland, as quoted in Cleveland County Council Report CR 573, *Impact of Unemployment on Individuals, Families and Communities* (1986c).
3. See the report by the Economist Ingelligence Unit (1982) *Britain's Jobless*.
4. An unemployed person in Cleveland. See note 2 for reference.
5. A 27-year-old unemployed man talking about his children. See note 2 for reference.
6. A very useful article on how families cope on supplementary benefit is 'Budgeting on benefit' by Jonathan Bradshaw and Jane Morgan in *New Society*, 6 March 1987.
7. A 1981 report for the Institute For Manpower Studies, summarised in Oswald and Turnbull (1985).
8. R. Berthoud (1984) *The Reform of Supplementary Benefit*, Policy Studies Institute.
9. This is the Breadline Britain Survey conducted for London Weekend Television and published as *Poor Britain* by Lansley and Mack (1985).
10. 29-year-old in Cleveland; see note 2.
11. 37-year-old in Cleveland; see note 2.

12. Unemployed person in Cleveland; see note 2.
13. Reported in R. Smith (1985) 'We get on each other's nerves — unemployment and the family', *British Medical Journal*, 291, pp. 1707–1710. Also reported in 'The human costs of unemployment', *Charter for Jobs Economic Report*, October 1986, Vol. 2. No. 1.
14. The 12-item General Health Questionnaire asks 12 questions which, when used for statistical analysis, offer a simple and reliable method of predicting a proneness to psychological ill health. See Appendix 1 to the report referenced in note 2.
15. This is *The Health Divide* published in March 1987 by the now defunct Health Education Council.
16. This is the study by Banks and Jackson (1982), referred to in the reports mentioned in notes 13 and 15.
17. This is the study by Moser, Fox and Jones (1984). See the reports mentioned in notes 13 and 15.
18. These studies are listed in the *Charter for Jobs Report* referred to in note 13.
19. 'Unemployment, school leaving and crime', Farrington *et al.* (1986), in the *British Journal of Criminology*, Vol. 26, No. 4.
20. A mother of an unemployed son and the wife of an unemployed husband, as quoted in Foord *et al.* (1985).
21. See an article by Peter Kellner, 'Awakening anger over the jobless', in *The Independent*, 27 April 1987.
22. See note 3.
23. I am grateful to David Ryder at Cleveland Social Services Department for sparking my thinking on this point.

The Response

5
The Invisible Hand

'When I worked in London that's anonymous-ville. People here have either always worked here, or moved away for a short period and come back. Many people say, "why should we have to leave here, why can't the government do something about the economic prospects so that prosperity doesn't end north of Watford?"'[1]

In Chapter 2 we drew attention to the weaknesses of traditional regional policy with its focus upon the attraction of branch plants and the doubts about its cost-effectiveness. In the following chapter we shall investigate how regional policy has been reformed by the post-1979 administration and how the government has developed its policies for the inner city. In this chapter we want to look at the notion that regional disparities in unemployment could be reduced by relying on market forces — the economist's invisible hand — which would involve removing the barriers which seem to hinder the operation of free markets.

What we are referring to is the 'Clarke—Lawson—Ridley' strategy for promoting regional economic development.[2] This strategy has two major components to it. Firstly, pay rates in labour markets with high unemployment would be reduced, relative to pay in more prosperous labour markets, with the aim of inducing workers to move away from the higher unemployment areas. In addition, it is hoped that firms would have more of an incentive to set up or expand in high unemployment areas if labour costs were lower. Secondly, business rates would be reduced in depressed labour markets, relative to more prosperous markets, as an additional incentive to firms to expand in or migrate to high-unemployment areas. The strategy would rely on the proposed reform of the rates to be introduced in England and Wales towards the end of the 1980s, and the breaking down of traditional national pay bargaining and barriers to labour mobility. The strategy therefore raises a set of empirical questions, such as what is the effect of business rates on employment, what is the influence of pay on firms and what is the evidence on the extent of, and the barriers to, labour mobility between regions?

The Clarke—Lawson—Ridley strategy is not exactly original. During the 1930s the mass migration of workers from the depressed areas to the South and the Midlands was advocated as the only solution to the problems of heavy regional unemployment. It was the outbreak of war, which boosted demand for labour in the regions, and the immediate post-war emphasis on active regional policy to steer work to the workers, which ended the interest in labour mobility. It has been resurrected in the 1980s because of disillusionment with regional policy, the explosion in unemployment and the emphasis upon labour market imperfections as the root cause of unemployment.

We shall focus first on regional pay differentials.[3] It would be a mistake to paint a portrait of a very rigid system of national pay determination, for although minimum pay rates are often set nationally, regional earnings can vary quite substantially because of local 'topping-up' of national rates. ICI is an interesting example in that it *combines* national pay bargaining with some local flexibility, as do most of the retailers (Marks and Spencer, Sainsburys), the banks and building societies, and the motor companies. These (very successful) companies emphasise the importance of national pay rates as being simple to administer, conducive to good industrial relations and an *aid* to internal company mobility, as employees are not put off by having to move to areas where pay is generally lower. Indeed, the private sector is distinctly unenthusiastic about ending national pay bargaining and, needless to say, the trade unions are bitterly hostile.

In Chapter 10 we shall review the evidence that firms might in fact heavily discount lower labour costs and would not be induced to increase their recruitment if pay *were* reduced in the assisted areas. This could be because the prejudice against the perceived image of 'the North', described in Chapter 3, is so deeply ingrained that modest variations in pay between the north and south have no effect. The Clark—Lawson—Ridley strategy gives no indication as to what *size* of regional pay differential is required: does relative pay in 'the North' have to fall by 5 per cent, 10 per cent, or should it be halved? Would it be wise to promote only low-paid, low-productivity jobs in 'the North', while concentrating the highly-paid, high-productivity jobs in 'the South', which has already been one of the perverse results of regional policy? If more firms are to locate in 'the North', would it not be necessary to pay senior managers and highly skilled workers *greater* salaries to induce them to move to areas which have an unfavourable image? And if these imported managers were paid significantly more than locally recruited labour, what would be the consequences for industrial relations?

How does the government propose to alter traditional patterns of bargaining? It seems unlikely that mere exhortation will change the minds of private employers and unions; indeed, ministers have tried the tactic of talking down wage increases for several years with no success whatsoever. It is likely that the government will try to alter attitudes in the public sector, but this could simply add further tension to an industrial relations scene already poisoned by the relative decline in public-sector pay and the apparent contempt shown by ministers towards those people working in the public sector. It is not at all clear, then, that the government has the faintest idea how to bring about greater differentiation in regional pay even if the evidence suggested this to be a wise move. Indeed, we run into the thundering paradox that, for private market forces to work in the manner which ministers would like to see, we would require more, not less, state intervention in order to break the traditional patterns of British pay bargaining.

The last comprehensive survey which looked specifically at labour mobility is now a quarter of a century out of date and we have to rely on more general information which comes from surveys where mobility is only one of many things being investigated.[4] Only 15 per cent of house movements are undertaken for job reasons; the rest are motivated by the desire to obtain more appropriate housing. Most job moves do not involve a change in house as they are moves within, rather than between, local labour markets. Most house movements are over very short distances, the vast majority involving a move no more than ten kilometres from the previous location. Thus most mobility is actually quite irrelevant to the unemployment question. During the recession, geographical mobility fell by about one-quarter in Britain as a whole. The net outflow of people from Cleveland increased slightly during the recession, but this was a consequence of fewer people coming to live in the county rather than more people leaving it.[5] It is clear therefore that labour migration is not part of any self-correcting market mechanism, for mobility falls when unemployment rises. What information we have suggests that geographical mobility has recovered since 1983, in line with the resumption in modest economic growth.

Labour migration is extremely selective. It is mainly the young, the well educated and skilled who migrate, while older, less skilled people are significantly less likely to move. Housing tenure is also an important influence, with council tenants four times less likely to move than owner-occupiers, who in turn are much less likely to move than people in the private rented sector.[6] What poor evidence we have suggests that the older, long-term unemployed in high unemployment areas are the least likely to move.[7] It would appear to be the case that it is the *pull* of job opportunities to those young educated people who are often already employed which influences mobility, rather than the *push* of unemployment. This process might reduce unemployment in an area where people are leaving through the release of jobs previously held by the movers, but there is nothing automatic in this process. However, in the longer run this selective out-migration can prove very damaging to the depressed areas which are drained of the very people, the young and skilled, who are most likely to form new businesses. Firms are increasingly attracted to areas which can boast a pool of well skilled and educated young people. Selective out-migration makes an area even less attractive to such firms, while further enhancing the pulling power of southern labour markets. Rather than acting as a self-correcting mechanism, labour migration seems to worsen regional disparities in the long run, leaving the depressed area in a downward spiral of out-migration and an ever more unfavourable image.

The tabloid version of the Clarke−Lawson−Ridley strategy emphasises the problem of severe shortages of skilled labour in the prospering labour markets of the south, which can only be solved by moving skilled workers from the north to fill the vacancies. In fact, over half of all vacancies notified to job centres are filled within one week and in April 1986 the MSC estimated that there were only 5,535 vacancies throughout Britain which had not been filled for two months because of skill shortages.[8] Only about one-third of vacancies are notified to the MSC, but this would still imply only 15−20,000 unfilled vacancies nationally which can be blamed on skill shortages, though unfortunately this can still feed 15−20,000 tabloid press reports (or indeed significantly more, given that the papers usually poach stories off each other). In the south-east region of England there were, according to the Labour Force survey, some 700,000 unemployed individuals in 1986, including a third of a million in Greater London, and there is no local labour market in the country where adjusted vacancies exceed unemployment. If there are 15,000 vacancies unfilled in the south-east, why not take 15,000 unemployed south-easterners (about 2 per cent of the total) and train them, so that they can fill the jobs? Economists tend to moan about those employers who poach workers from other firms, rather than invest in training and so enhance the stock of skills available in the whole economy. Then the same economists advocate that 'the South' poach skilled workers from 'the North' rather than train the huge numbers of unskilled, unemployed southerners.

There are some very important barriers which hinder the whole process of labour migration of which the most important are poor information, social ties and above all housing. In Cleveland, the main source of intelligence about job opportunities comes from informal information networks, rather than through the official job centres. Of course, migration cuts one off from these informal information networks, while it is extremely difficult to tap into these networks in the destination area. The main binding social ties would appear to be the schooling of the children and the employment of the spouse.[9]

It is the housing barrier which receives most attention. The form of tenure which most promotes mobility is private rented accommodation which has been in decline in Britain (and some other countries) for half a century. This has been the outcome of controls over the rents which can be charged in the private sector and the enormous fiscal subsidies available to the owner-occupied sector which results in rented accommodation being sold into owner-occupation as soon as tenants leave. To emphasise rent controls, without pointing to the impact of these subsidies, is to offer a very incomplete argument. Movement within the owner-occupied sector is made increasingly difficult by the growing gulf in house prices between 'the North' and 'the South'. This is the outcome of a demand for housing in the south which is artificially inflated by easy credit, booming incomes and tax reliefs, running into a supply of housing constrained by planning controls and green-belt legislation. Local authority housing can make no contribution to the problem because of its scarcity in the southern labour markets and the difficulty in getting councils to reserve some proportion of their stock for outsiders.

To get some idea of the financial costs involved in moving between regions, it is worth noting that British Telecom spends £8,000–£23,000 on each employee it moves, and the CBI reports that figures of up to £50,000 in subsidy from firms for relocating employees is not uncommon.[10] In total, private firms spend some £250 million a year promoting resettlement for 30,000 key employees. Most firms expect some of this subsidy to be repaid and draw up contracts to ensure that workers do not leave the company after taking advantage of the subsidy. Therefore, in promoting geographical mobility, these private relocation schemes make mobility *between* firms less likely. There is also another paradox to note in the housing market. Capital gains tax is not payable on the sale of houses and this means that southern managers and skilled workers are unwilling to move north to take advantage of lower house prices because they are afraid of losing out on the appreciation in the value of their houses in the south.[11]

Many economists ask why the government does not offset these migration costs through the use of public subsidies. The blunt answer is that just such an approach has been tried, but that the mix of schemes run by the MSC since the 1970s was scrapped wholesale in 1986 because it just could not be made to work.[12] The Employment Transfer Scheme offered a travel grant and assistance with removal and legal costs to help the unemployed, who could not otherwise move, fill vacancies which could not be filled in the local labour market. The unemployed had to show that there were no vacancies they could fill in their local labour market, while the employer had to show that he had tried and failed to attract suitable local labour. These criteria, which were in themselves expensive to administer, still did not prevent 'deadweight', with the MSC estimating that about half of the unemployed using the subsidy would have moved anyway. The MSC also estimated that between one and two thirds of the jobs filled under the scheme could have been filled locally, so that migrants were simply displacing the unemployed in the receiving areas. Many of those who moved did not remain long in their new jobs but drifted back home. The MSC abandoned this and similar subsidies and now has a simplified Travel-to-Interview Scheme which helps defray the transport costs involved in attending interviews held beyond normal daily travelling distance.

It should also be emphasised that the far more aggressive labour mobility programmes which have been a feature of Swedish labour market policy have run into problems, not least that assisted migrants tended not to stay in their original destination areas and over one third drifted home.[13] OECD data suggest that mobility has fallen significantly in Sweden, France, Germany, Norway and Japan during the 1980s, yet of course unemployment rates diverge enormously in these countries.[14] Mobility does not appear to have fallen in either the United States or Canada, but the unemployment rates of these two countries have recently diverged quite considerably, after years of moving together. Clearly, there is no correlation internationally between levels of, or trends in, geographical mobility and trends in unemployment. The assertion that the US labour force is especially mobile has been doubted by the MSC itself on the basis of survey evidence.[15] Moreover, the crucial difference in American and British mobility is that the former is *not* selective, in fact manual workers in the US are *more* likely to move than non-manual workers.[16]

The conclusion of Lord Young's submission to the National Economic Development Council in October 1986 was that '. . . it would be wrong to suppose that a higher level of mobility would lead to a major reduction in unemployment, though it might have some effect at the margin.'[17] This indicates that one senior cabinet minister at least doubts the validity of the Clarke–Lawson–Ridley strategy. The second leg of that strategy is the depressing of business rates in the north in order to attract firms and improve employment. However, 'the overwhelming weight of the theoretical and empirical evidence . . . casts doubt on the importance of the level of local taxes in Britain for local economic development.'[18] This result will be surprising to many people, given the enormous political interest in local rates, but this interest does not seem to be a function of the results of serious research, but a function of the political capital which can apparently be made out of pressing the issue along with the general alleged incompetence of local authorities.

The point of economic theory that has to be grasped is that the agent who is formally charged with a tax does not necessarily pay the tax: he may pass it on to someone else (in the jargon, the formal incidence of the tax may not equal the true incidence). So VAT is charged on businesses, but of course they merely pass it on to customers, by and large. Likewise, in theory, business rates can be passed on to customers or passed back to the owners of land through lower rents.

There is now a great deal of circumstantial evidence that a major part of the burden of local taxes is passed back to rent takers. In the Enterprise Zones (such as those in Middlesbrough and Hartlepool) which we will look at in the next chapter, rates are not charged at all on businesses for the first ten years — a significant incentive, one would think. But rents and land values in the Zones appear to have risen sharply when compared with those for equivalent premises and sites in the surrounding area. Other research assembles evidence for London suggesting that rent differentials tend to even out variations in local rates, so that there is a relatively standard 'composite' price for industrial space in London

(excluding the most and least favoured locations) despite the wide variations in rates payable.[19] This research also shows that local taxes in Britain are in fact quite small in relation to profits and turnover. Using 1980
Census of Production figures, rates paid were equivalent to only 0.6 per
cent of gross output value of manufacturing industry and 4.3 per cent
of gross profits. This is considerably less than in the United States.
A survey of plant relocation found that only about 10 per cent of firms
in London cited lower rates among their reasons for moving.[20] A study
undertaken for the Joint Economic Committee of the US Congress in
1979 indicated only a weak relationship between local taxes and the willingness of firms to invest or remain in inner-city areas. Local government's *attitude* to business was rated more highly than the level of local
taxes per se.[21] Another extensive piece of research failed to detect any
link between the rate of change of rate burdens and changes in employment in Britain.[22]

The conclusion appears quite clear. The part of the Clarke−Lawson−
Ridley strategy designed to encourage firms to move to areas with lower
rates (in the north) will be largely offset by the higher rents caused by
the shifting of tax incidence. For some inner London authorities and councils like Liverpool, it is their perceived hostile attitudes to private enterprise which are probably damaging, not high business rates.

So what is left of the Clarke−Lawson−Ridley strategy? The evidence
is very strong that the focus on business rates is a red herring. Even
if lower labour costs did lead to an expansion in employment in the
assisted areas, the strategy has no instruments for bringing this about.
Increased geographical mobility is mostly irrelevant so long as the
numbers of unemployed in the south so greatly outweigh any vacancies
and such mobility would further damage the long-run prospects of the
assisted areas. Instead, we want to put the focus on education and training to enhance the total stock of skills in the economy and allow those
most disadvantaged in the labour markets, both north and south, to compete more effectively for any jobs which are available. In looking at the
reform of housing policy (as we will in Chapter 11) there are many issues
to consider, but promoting labour mobility is not the most significant
one by any means.

Notes

1. A local government officer in Cleveland, quoted in Foord *et al.* (1985),
   p. 61.

2. Named after the former Employment minister, the Chancellor, and the Environment Secretary who are most closely associated with it.
3. We are drawing on the note by the Chancellor and the Employment Secretary on 'Regional Pay Variations', delivered to the NEDC on 25 November 1986, and on the Memorandum from the Trades Union Congress delivered at the same time.
4. The large-scale survey on mobility was the Government Social Survey of Labour Mobility in Great Britain, 1953–63. More recent information can be gained from the General Household and Labour Force surveys.
5. This is based on information from Cleveland County Council using the population census.
6. See the articles by Hughes and McCormick (1981, 1985 and 1987). Council tenants are not less likely to consider the possibility of migration, only less likely to be able to migrate.
7. See Daniel (1974). See also the general review of evidence on labour mobility contained in Green *et al.* (1986).
8. See *Department of Employment Gazette*, April 1987.
9. This is emphasised in an annex presented by the CBI to the NEDC on 24 October 1986.
10. See the annex referred to in note 9.
11. This was pointed out to the author by David Storey.
12. See the annex prepared by the MSC for the NEDC meeting referred to in note 9. See also Beaumont (1976).
13. Johannesson and Persson-Tanimura (1978), Swedish Ministry of Labour. My thanks to Richard Jackman for drawing my attention to this.
14. See annex 1 on 'Geographical Mobility' prepared for the NEDC meeting referred to in note 9.
15. See the November 1985 *Quarterly Report* from the MSC, 'Labour market flexibility in the United States of America'.
16. See Hughes and McCormick (1987).
17. See the paper presented by the Employment Secretary to the NEDC, 24 October 1986.
18. See Kirwan, 'Local fiscal policy and inner city economic development', Ch. 6, in Hausner (1986), p. 205. This section on the effects of business rates draws almost exclusively on Kirwan's tremendous summary of the evidence.
19. See Tyler *et al.* (1986).
20. Carried out for the Greater London Council, 1983. See Kirwan, p. 204.
21. See Kirwan, p. 204.
22. Fothergill *et al.* (1984).

6
The New Regional Policy

'Given the substantial powers, the tidal flow of public money and above all the location, we could not possibly have failed.'[1]

The government which came to power in 1979 was hostile to the whole concept of regional policy, which was after all just another facet of the state interference in the workings of private markets which the government was pledged to roll back. Traditional regional policy has indeed been curtailed, but its place has been taken by a confusing plethora of other initiatives: Enterprise Zones (EZs), Urban Development Corporations (UDCs), City Action Task Forces (CATFs), and so on. Indeed, one is reminded of the so-called 'alphabet agencies' of Roosevelt's New Deal in the 1930s, when organisations like the TVA and NRA spearheaded a new era of state intervention in the US economy. Even institutions like the Scottish Development Agency which were set up by the previous Labour administration have been given a new lease of life. So much for free markets!

In Chapter 2 we were quite sympathetic to many of the criticisms which have been made of traditional regional policy, the doubts about its cost-effectiveness, its heavy focus on attracting branch plants and its neglect of service industries, marketing and research and development activities. In 1984 the government finally came around to a wholesale reform of regional policy, building upon some piecemeal changes which had been instituted since 1979.[2] Already, restrictions on industrial development in the south, designed to steer plants to the assisted areas, had been abolished. Now a series of reforms was introduced to improve cost-effectiveness and cut overall expenditure. The areas which could benefit from automatic regional development grants (RDGs) were restricted and the top rate of grant was reduced from 22 per cent to 15 per cent. A cost-per-job limit of £10,000 was imposed on RDGs and much more attention was to be placed on discretionary Regional Selective Assistance (RSA). Replacement or modernisation investment was no longer eligible for RDGs and RSA was to be used to protect existing jobs as well as create new ones. Certain service industries could now claim assistance including finance, business services, research and development and marketing. The map of regional assistance was redrawn to focus aid on more tightly defined areas and to bring in the West Midlands as an area eligible for RSA, reflecting its decline from growth zone to trouble spot (Figure 6.1).

Expenditure on regional policy has been more than halved in real terms from £822 million in 1981–82 to £408 million in 1985–86. Many analysts have suggested that central government has more or less given up on the instrument of regional policy, returning full circle to the 1930s when it was seen as a social palliative rather than a serious contribution to achieving a resurgence of economic prosperity in the assisted areas. Nevertheless, it is hard to criticise many of the details of the reform package, particularly the emphasis on avoiding the subsidising of rationalisation projects such as those at BSC, which may be necessary if firms are to remain competitive, but is inappropriate as a target for regional policies which, in a recession, need to focus upon job creation as a primary aim. The inclusion of service industries is sensible, as is the whole emphasis on cost-effectiveness in delivering assistance. As yet, there have been no evaluations of the impact of this reformed regional policy, but the impression is gathering that the remaining incentives are heavily discounted by most firms, few of which seem likely to relocate their manufacturing or service activities to the assisted areas.

If traditional regional policy has been serverely restricted, its place has been taken by the 'alphabet agencies'. The most interesting of these institutions is the Scottish Development Agency (SDA) which was set up in 1975 to provide a focus for coordinating urban and industrial development in central Scotland. Despite being an interventionist body it was not scrapped after 1979, thus avoiding the old cliché that each incoming government always abolishes whatever new agencies were set up by the previous government. If Cleveland could claim the title of the jewel in the crown of 1960s regional policy, then Scotland appears to be the jewel of the new regional policy. The SDA is now talked about enthusiastically by government ministers (and ex-ministers, notably Michael Heseltine) and by Labour and Alliance spokesmen, and the

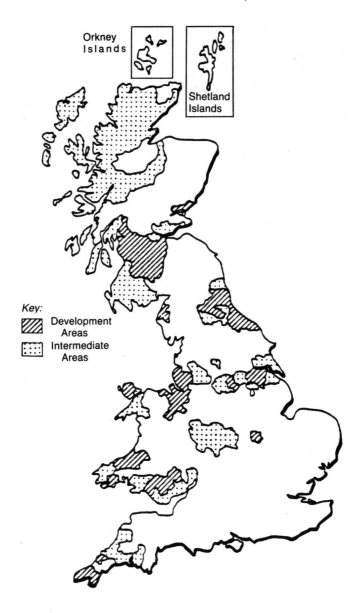

Figure 6.1 The British Assisted Areas at November 1984

opposition parties would like to see similar agencies set up in the English regions. This sounds like an impressive consensus, but does it reflect a sober analysis of the performance of the SDA and its applicability to the problems of the English regions?

Central Scotland bears striking similarities to the North-East of England in terms of its coal-based past and its pattern of industrial and urban decay. The achievement of the SDA is seen to lie both in its urban programmes, specifically the Glasgow Eastern Area Renewal (GEAR) initiative and its construction of a new base of hi-tech industries in the so-called 'Silicon Glen' between Glasgow and Edinburgh.

To take Silicon Glen first, it is true that over 40,000 people are now employed in the electronics sector in Scotland.[3] However, Silicon Glen owes its existence partly to historical accident, when the first Ferranti factory was set up in the Second World War to manufacture bomb sights for the RAF in a safe location out of the range of the Luftwaffe. About 40 per cent of employment in this sector is in US multinationals and most of the rest is in English-owned firms, with the leading eight US and English companies employing about half the workforce in Silicon Glen. Less than 10 per cent of employment is in Scottish-owned firms, most of whom are subcontractors to the larger multinationals. There is a heavy concentration of activity in the manufacture of basic semi-conductors and personal computers, where there is a growing threat from countries such as Taiwan and South Korea. There is relatively little Research and Development activity and surprisingly few well-developed links with the offshore industry. The multinationals purchase few of their components locally, and often from each other, rather than Scottish-owned firms. Most of the employment offered is not highly skilled and over half the workforce is female. What Silicon Glen is not is an obvious example of tremendous Scottish entrepreneurship and its expansion has not compensated for the decline in male manufacturing jobs in Glasgow and the coalfields. It is in fact a classic branch-plant economy.

The GEAR initiative was one of a series of programmes launched in the 1970s to focus the attention of public policy on the inner-city problem. It took the SDA some time to develop a strategy and overcome the political frictions which marred the early days of the initiative. One half of the strategy was aimed at improvements to the physical environment in order to enhance the image of the area, with the initial impetus coming from public investment, followed by some modest injections of private capital in housing developments. The other half of the strategy

— economic regeneration to provide employment — has been less successful, with the GEAR area suffering badly from the recession. The new service jobs which have been brought to the area have provided much employment (of the low-paid and low-skilled variety) to labour market entrants, but few jobs have gone to the long-term unemployed and, in common with all area initiatives, many of the jobs have leaked to outside commuters.

So far we have painted a less-than-fully-complementary picture of the SDA, and this is perhaps a little unfair. The virtue of the SDA is that it learns from its mistakes and sets an example to the private sector in being a rigorously managed and well organised institution, which pays attention to constantly re-evaluating its role and programmes.[4] Nevertheless, it is wise to be circumspect when analysing the performance of the agency and not to oversell its attributes. The Scottish economy has seen a somewhat less serious upsurge in unemployment when compared with, say, Cleveland, but it is hard to disentangle the effect of the SDA from the benefits provided by offshore activity. The collapse in oil prices in 1986 could cost Scotland up to 33,000 jobs by 1988, bringing its unemployment rate much closer to that in the north of England.[5]

It is not at all clear that the SDA is an institution which could be easily transferred to the English regions.[6] Scotland is a relatively homogeneous nation with a clear sense of national identity and a greater degree of self-confidence. Regional identity is not so nearly well developed in England. An individual is more likely to refer to himself as originating from Cornwall, Manchester or Nottingham, rather than the South-West, the North-West or the East Midlands. The Northern Region is a little more cohesive, but there are still felt to be differences between Tyneside, Teesside and, certainly, Cumbria. Most English people identify with a city or town or perhaps a county, but rarely a region. This is an important point to stress for it could lead to friction within any regional body, with a 'Northern Development Agency' pulled by disparate forces and too clearly identified with Newcastle, to the disadvantage of Teesside or industrial West Cumbria. Even the SDA has been accused of being the 'Strathclyde Development Agency' because of its alleged bias towards that part of Scotland.

Scotland has the only real independent financial sector outside London, a distinctive legal system and an independent education system which produces a high proportion of science and engineering graduates.[7] It has a strong voice in the Scottish Office (with a seat in Cabinet) and it is to this body that the SDA is answerable. The North simply does not have the same political. administrative or institutional infrastructure. It is not clear that a regional body could carry out functions better than reformed local authorities, which are more likely to be responsive to local feeling than regional agencies, which could prove as remote as Whitehall and would be answerable to, and have their priorities dictated by, Whitehall.

In early 1987 a consortium of 160 private firms, some trade unions and the local authorities, joined together to form a Northern Development Company (NDC) with mixed private–public funding. This body exemplifies a 'bottom-up' approach to regional development, rather than relying on a Whitehall-imposed initiative, and this is to be thoroughly welcomed. The SDA has focused attention on the need to promote consensus and partnership between the private and public sectors and project a favourable image to help promote inward investment.[8] This political and marketing role would seem to be what the NDC is best suited for, but we will develop the case in Chapter 9 for leaving many other activities in the hands of reformed local authorities.[9]

Cleveland has two Enterprise Zones (in Middlesbrough and Hartlepool) and a city action task force in north-central Middlesbrough and, from 1987, a Teesside urban development corporation will be set up. The UDC will cover some 3,500 acres along the banks of the River Tees, including some of the worst urban and industrial dereliction in Europe. It will encompass in its boundaries the Middlesbrough EZ and CATF. It will be possible for one firm to have access simultaneously to the benefits of the EZ, the CATF, the UDC, RDGs and RSA, the various funding initiatives available under the Urban Programme (UP), Urban Development Grants (UDGs), Urban Regeneration Grants (URGs), and various grants available from the European Community, not to mention the services available from English Estates. RDGs, RSA and the CATF are run by the Department of Trade and Industry (DTI), the UDC, the EZs and the UP by the Department of Environment (DoEn) with additional input from the Departments of Employment and Education and the Manpower Services Commission.

The main argument advanced by Whitehall for imposing central initiatives like the UDC is that the local authorities have overlapping responsibilities, squabble and do not present a clear and understandable front to private firms! The proliferation of alphabet agencies took the author six months to track down (and I still think I missed a few). It is quite accurate to criticise the local authorities in Cleveland for the poor coordination of their activities. This has been the inevitable outcome of a two-tier system of local government which is entirely inappropriate to

Teesside (as we shall see again in Chapter 11). However, it is not at all clear that the imposition of numerous alphabet agencies, all run by different Whitehall departments (which are even more notorious for squabbling), achieves anything except to further compound a confusing and debilitating administrative and financial mess.

For the moment we shall concentrate on the economic case for some of these initiatives. The Enterprise Zones were instituted in 1980 and offer a ten-year period during which firms are not charged rates and, in addition, planning procedures are relaxed. However, we noted in the last chapter that land rentals appear to adjust more or less fully to differences in rates so that this incentive is by no means as strong as many people might think. The 190-acre Brittania Enterprise Zone in Middlesbrough had 700 people employed in 65 establishments by September 1984.[10] However, 600 people and 48 establishments were already working in the zone when it was designated in November 1983. National evidence suggests that only one in eight firms setting up in EZs appears to owe its existence to the benefits available in these areas.[11] The vast majority of jobs created in the EZs would probably have been created anyway and in nearby locations. The zones appear to have mainly shuffled jobs around a little and at considerable cost in rate revenues lost. In fact, the EZs appear to have suffered to a greater degree from the very problems which are said to have plagued traditional regional policy and of which the post-1979 administration was so critical, most notably cost-ineffectiveness.

The model for the Teesside UDC is of course the London Docklands Development Corporation (LDDC) which has joined the SDA in being trumpeted as the best thing since sliced bread. The UDCs have full planning powers in the areas in which they operate and not just over any publicly-owned land, but all privately-owned land, too. These socialist planning institutions are funded by central government on an annual basis and as such are subject to the vagaries of public expenditure controls. The Teesside UDC will have £100−160 million pumped into it over six or seven years and it is hoped that this public money will serve to lever complementary private funds. The LDDC has been the recipient of over £300 million of public money since its inception in 1981 and the 'leverage ratio' appears to have been in the order of 4:1, so that each pound of public money has attracted at least four pounds from the private sector. The equivalent ratio in the Merseyside Development Corporation has been 1:7, so that every seven pounds of public money has attracted one pound from the private sector. The Merseyside UDC has thus been one twenty-eighth as successful as the LDDC.[12]

Is Teesside likely to perform as well as London or as poorly as Merseyside? Clearly, it could not hope to emulate the success of the LDDC, as is recognised in the quote with which we began this chapter, which attributes the success of the LDDC above all to its location, and this really should come as a surprise to no-one. There is no Fleet Street, nor big financial institutions ready to move into Teesside, and few private-sector bodies are likely to invest large sums of capital.

In fact, at second glance, the LDDC is by no means the great success it is claimed to be. Over 6,000 homes have already been completed, but nearly all of them have gone to outsiders, the 'yuppies' who can afford to pay the spiralling property prices. The majority of traditional Docklands residents earn less than £10,000 per annum because of low pay or unemployment, but house prices *start* at £40,000 and are therefore beyond the reach of most local people. Likewise, employment has been brought to the Docklands but very few of the jobs have gone to residents. There has instead been an influx of commuters. So the LDDC has brought 'development', but *who* is supposed to benefit from it? The main beneficiaries have been the owners of property, the builders, and middle-class people who already have jobs. The traditional working-class residents, the council tenants and the unemployed have been by-passed by this initiative, just as they have been by-passed by the economic recovery as a whole.

The North-Central Middlesbrough Task Force was set up in February 1986 precisely because of the realisation that existing government programmes were failing to target and benefit the very local communities which were supposed to be the beneficiaries. It has a budget of one million pounds to cover an area where some 15,000 people are out of work, but its main impact is supposed to be achieved by better targeting of existing programmes which the Task Force hopes to coordinate. The key objective is to help local people into existing or new jobs, which is precisely the kind of targeting which we are advocating. However, there are doubts over whether the initiative will survive after March 1988, especially as the task force area is to be subsumed by the Teesside UDC. Any local avenues of communication and intelligence and any trust and skills which may have been built up will then be lost. This rams home a more general point that the constant turnover of alphabet agencies, programmes and the people who run them, means that any worthwhile initiatives are not sustained, and the lessons which are learned are lost again. Most of the task force staff had not been in their jobs for more than a short while and had not been given the chance to build the necessary skills and contacts which are vital if employment initiatives are to reach those people in most need. The task force is accountable to Whitehall, with each of its projects having to be vetted by the relevant minister! Is that minister so familiar with local needs and sensibilities that he is qualified to pass judgement on what will work and what will not?

Although the economic principle on which the task force operates (targeted employment) is precisely correct, it is not the best administrative agency to put that principle into practice. For surely the targeting of jobs on local communities requires local organisations which are locally accountable. Central government has organised a plethora of schemes which seem to by-pass local government because local government is alleged to be inefficiently organised and in some cases hostile to private enterprise. In fact, only a very few local authorities are hostile and if they are sometimes inefficient, this is a reflection of their organisation under the Local Government Act, their electoral base and administrative procedures and the perverse incentives created by the existing central controls on local authorities. We will develop further in Chapter 9 the thesis that if there is something wrong with local government, the correct response is the root and branch reform of local government, not the imposition of further central control which removes any incentive for a local authority to improve.

This chapter has tried to suggest that, while traditional regional policy has been demoted, its replacement — the alphabet agencies — is not performing well. The two main problems we have identified are, firstly, the confusion and overlap in administration and, secondly, the fact that the agencies are not targeting those people who should benefit most from any government initiative: the individuals and communities who are being by-passed by the economic recovery. However, the impact of both the traditional and the new form of regional policy is quite small when compared to the impact of the greatest of the alphabet agencies — the MSC.

Notes

1. Board member of the London Docklands Development Corporation, quoted in *The Financial Times*, 13 May 1987.
2. See the White Paper on Regional Industrial Development, Command 9111,

HMSO. Chapter 7 of Armstrong and Taylor (1986) gives an excellent short summary of the reforms.
3. The best sources of information on the SDA and the 'Silicon Glen' phenomenon are Moore and Booth (1986), Lever and Moore (1986) and the '1986 Review of the Scottish Development Aency: Summary Report' from the Industry Department for Scotland, Edinburgh.
4. This is stressed by the report referred to in note 3 from the Scottish Industry Department.
5. See Salomond and Walker (1986).
6. This appears to be recognised by the head of the SDA, George Matthewson. See *The Financial Times*, 7 November 1986. It is also the case which is persuasively argued by Moore and Booth (1986).
7. It should be noted that Wales lacks all of these things and the Welsh Development Agency (WDA) has been conspicuously less successful than its Scottish counterpart.
8. The contrast is with Liverpool, whose local authority developed a reputation for xenophobic militancy.
9. The attraction of inward investment is an especially important task for a regional body, so as to avoid zero-sum competition between local authorities all competing for a fixed number of mobile plants.
10. See p. 46 of Foord *et al.* (1985).
11. See Roger Tym and Partners (1984) and Botham and Lloyd (1984).
12. See 'The two-faced phoenix' by Hazel Duffy in *The Financial Times*, 13 May 1987. See also *The Financial Times* 'Survey on urban renewal', 6 October 1986.

7
The MSC: Manpower Services Commission or Ministers' Social Conscience?

'We can do a great deal but at the end of the day there are not enough jobs.'[1]

'The future? Waiting for the next CP·scheme, I suppose.'[2]

The government which came to power in 1979 was not obviously sympathetic to special employment and training measures and to the 'corporatist quango' which was responsible for administering them. Indeed, it was considered likely that the Manpower Services Commission, which had been created in 1973 to bring together the running of the job centres and adult training, would be chopped as part of the drive against Civil Service numbers and the proliferation of administrative agencies. In fact, the government will spend £3,000 million in 1987−8 on employment and training measures, most of it through the MSC, which now has a staff of around 25,000, making it one of the largest administrative bodies in the country. The Department of Employment Group, which includes the MSC, has seen the fastest proportionate rate of growth in expenditure of any part of government.

In May 1979 there were about a quarter of a million people covered by various special measures, chiefly the Youth Opportunities Programme (the precursor to the Youth Training Scheme) and various employment subsidies which were being used either to save or create jobs (Table 7.1). By June 1983 the numbers covered by special measures had grown by nearly 200,000, with over half the growth accounted for by the expansion of the Youth Opportunities Programme, which in September 1983 would be superseded by the new one-year Youth Training Scheme (YTS). By February 1987 more than a quarter of a million additional places had been provided, reflecting the growth of the YTS, the quadrupling of

Table 7.1 The Growth in Special Employment Measures, 1979−87

	May 1979	June 1983	February 1987	1987−8 (projected)
Youth Opportunities Programme/ Youth Training Scheme	(66,000)	(188,400)	327,900	362,000
Community Programme	(14,500)	64,000	247,000	245,000
Job Training Scheme	—	—	1,500	110,000
New/Young Workers Scheme	—	103,000	34,200	51,000
Enterprise Allowance	—	—	78,000	110,000
Community Industry	(5,300)	8,000	6,880	8,000
Other employment subsidies	108,000	22,000	—	—
Job Release Scheme	24,200	81,000	25,000	26,000
Job Splitting Scheme	—	500	270	1,000
Jobstart Allowance	—	—	—	20,000
Total	(257,000)	444,900	720,750	933,000
Estimated register effect	—	304,800	545,700	(700,000)

places on the Community Programme (CP) aimed at the long-term unemployed, and the institution of the new Enterprise Allowance Scheme (EAS). In 1987−8 over 900,000 people are expected to be participating in special measures at any one time, with the growth in numbers largely accounted for by the new Job Training Scheme (JTS).

We suggested in Chapter 1 that the government was genuinely taken by surprise at the shattering growth in unemployment in the early 1980s. The expansion in the role and activities of the MSC was the most visible response that was possible, given the determination of the government not to be *seen* to perform a U-turn in reflating the economy. This is the explanation for our rather cynical chapter heading — the MSC as the 'Ministers' Social Conscience'. The rapid growth in the places provided under YOP during the first term of office and the institution of YTS can be seen as unplanned responses to the dramatic increase in youth unemployment in the 1980s, which was politically deeply unpopular. Ministers had to be seen to be doing something, especially as the public was linking youth unemployment to rising crime and inner-city unrest. The growth in the CP in the second term of office of the government can be seen as the response of ministerial conscience to the growth in the numbers of people out of work for long periods. Neither the 1979, nor the 1983 election manifestos foresaw the growth in these two programmes, so that the success of YTS and CP in reducing registered unemployment cannot be fairly claimed to be part of the government's original strategy for curing Britain's economic problems.

The MSC has also extended its interventionist role in the education system, through its Technical and Vocational Education Initiative (TVEI) and increased financial influence on non-advanced further education. This has led the MSC's critics in education to dub it rather unkindly the 'Ministry of Social Control'. This aspect of the Commission's activities and its youth and adult training strategies are discussed in Chapter 12, and in Chapter 9 we will look at the Enterprise Allowance Scheme. The focus of this chapter is on the programmes which have been aimed at the long-term unemployed: the Restart Initiative and, most importantly, the Community Programme. We shall take the six criteria outlined in Chapter 1 for judging employment programmes and apply them to the MSC schemes. Only after such a careful and rigorous analysis of their actual performance can we fairly say whether the MSC is making a valuable contribution to countering the unbalanced recovery or whether the MSC deserves its very unflattering joke title, often heard in the north of England, of 'Massive Social Con'.

Restart

In April 1987 the Restart Initiative was extended nationwide to provide special counselling for those people who have been out of work for more than six months and are registered unemployed. The idea is to provide a menu of options from which the unemployed can choose — a range of employment and training measures designed to help the long-term unemployed back into jobs. The initiative has been surrounded by controversy, both because of somewhat misleading presentations of its success rate by ministers and its alleged emphasis on reducing unemployment by scaring people off the register who are not genuinely unemployed. Once again we are unwilling to tread into the political and statistical minefield raised by the changes in the definition of unemployment and administrative practice which have been instituted since 1979. Instead, we want to focus upon the impact of Restart on the labour market.

The first thing to be emphasised is that 84 per cent of those who attend Restart interviews receive no concrete help whatsoever and return immediately to unemployment (Table 7.2). Less than one in a hundred actually obtains a job, and about 5 per cent go on to the CP, the EAS, or a training course. A very small number are steered into voluntary work and

Table 7.2　Destination of Restart Claimants (Interviewed 12 May
to 9 October)

Total interviewed	333,451	
Placed in:		
Jobs	2,547	(0.8%)
Community Programmes	9,757	(2.9%)
Job Clubs	2,508	(0.7%)
Enterprise Allowance	1,585	(0.5%)
Training	5,488	(1.6%)
Restart courses	31,012	(9.2%)
Voluntary Projects Programme	1,054	(0.3%)
Total helped	53,951	(16%)

about 10 per cent go on to Restart courses and Job Clubs which are designed to help them search more effectively for whatever jobs are available. Nevertheless, many people might consider even a 16 per cent success rate to be very good and a lot better than nothing. However, even these very limited results cannot be taken at face value.

The first problem is known in the jargon as *deadweight* — many of the people who obtained work or training might have done so anyway, without the assistance of Restart. It is misleading to think of the unemployed as a stagnant pool, for there are people becoming unemployed and ceasing to be unemployed every day. About four million people lose their jobs each year and a similar number find work again.[3] To note that some people who attend a Restart interview do get jobs is quite meaningless unless one can say that they would not have obtained jobs otherwise. In fact, Restart was planned and piloted so quickly that there is (in early 1987) no evidence as to whether the initiative genuinely raises a participant's chances of finding employment.

We can best investigate the problems surrounding Restart by looking at one of its components — the Job Clubs which were pioneered in Middlesbrough. The Clubs offer two weeks of free access to telephones and stationery and advice on job-hunting techniques, which are designed to help claimants make at least ten job applications each day. 1,000 Job Clubs were in place by April 1987 and in 1987–8 some 150,000 claimants are expected to pass through. Of 7,589 people who attended Job Clubs between September and December 1986, about three out of five found employment and another 13 per cent were given places on the CP, EAS or training schemes.[4] This sounds impressive, but is it?

First of all, there is the strong suspicion that most of the placements were deadweight, in that most of the participants would have found jobs anyway. This follows from an all-pervasive problem which is found with any government scheme such as this one — the phenomenon of 'creaming'.[5] Unemployed people can only join a Club by invitation from Job Centre staff and it can be seen from Table 7.1 that very few people actually get invited. Only long-term unemployed people with reading and writing skills are recruited, thus excluding the 350—400,000 who are estimated to have literacy problems. There is evidence that staff tend to recruit the most qualified people who have been unemployed for shorter periods rather than the unskilled who have been out of work for a very long time. So the Job Clubs are catering for the least disadvantaged of the unemployed, the people most likely to obtain jobs anyway.

Another problem is that of substitution — that the participants in Job Clubs may obtain employment only at the expense of other job seekers. It is strongly rumoured that participants obtain first look at any vacancies which are reported to Job Centres and most people remain in a Club *until* they obtain employment or drop out, so that claims of a high success rate appear somewhat vacuous. In effect the Job Clubs give the least unfortunate of the unemployed a huge competitive advantage over the rest in obtaining placements which they might have obtained anyway. There is no firm evidence to prove that the Clubs raise the chances of participants in finding work. Similar comments could be made about the Restart Courses, which are watered-down Job Clubs designed to give the unemployed skills in compiling a CV, writing job applications, handling interviews, and so on.

It would be unfair not to mention two possible benefits from the Restart Initiative. Firstly, it reverses several years of staff cuts at Job Centres with the recruitment of an additional 2,000 civil servants to cope with the Restart interviews. Secondly, many of the unemployed may have been unaware of the job or training opportunities which are available and Restart may help to plug this information gap. However, it is not at all clear that the interviews are being used to gather really detailed and specific information about the past employment and skills and future requirements of the unemployed, so that they can be carefully matched to whatever opportunities are available. We will consider further in Chapter 12 whether the MSC is performing its first task as a labour board as competently as it should.

The Community Programme

The CP is the main government programme aimed at the long-term unemployed and as such deserves serious and detailed attention. Adults who have been out of work for more than twelve months and people under twenty-five who have been out of work for over six months are eligible for the scheme. In early 1987 there were one and three quarter million people in the CP Client Group with a quarter of a million participants actually on the programme. Placements under the scheme usually last one year and the vast majority of projects are sponsored by local authorities and voluntary organisations, with negligible private-sector participation. In fact, the whole practice of the CP would seem to be completely at odds with government rhetoric, in that people are employed in public services, which are presumably just as much a drain on the wealth-generating private sector as all public services are supposed to be. The work which is performed must be of benefit to the community *but* should not substitute for work which would have been undertaken anyway within two years (the 'two-year rule') and any private gain must be incidental. Participants are paid the rate for the job, but the average maximum wage is limited to £67 per week which means that more than eight in ten participants work part-time, often for only 16 to 24 hours per week.

If we compare the characteristics of the CP participants with those unemployed people who are eligible, a very selective pattern of recruitment to the scheme reveals itself (Table 7.3). The balance between the sexes appears to be about right, but this is partly an illusion resulting from the exclusion of married women from the unemployment register.

Table 7.3 Characteristics of Community Programme Participants compared to Community Programme Client Group (%)

	CP participants	CP client group
Female	25.0	26.0
18–24-year-olds	62.0	37.0
45-year-olds and over	14.0	29.0
Unemployed over 2 years	24.0	50.0

The age composition of the CP is seriously skewed however, with nearly two-thirds of CP participants aged under twenty-five and the older long-term unemployed seriously under-represented, with less than half the places on the CP to which they should be entitled. It is also clear from Table 7.3 that the very long-term unemployed, those out of work for two years or more, make up only one quarter of CP participants, but one half of the client group. Since the scheme's inception, the number of very long-term unemployed, older people and those working full-time has fallen significantly so that the CP has increasingly become a part-time programme for young, single people who have not been out of work for as long.

Part of the explanation for this must be the low average wage.[6] Clearly, £67 per week is not attractive to a family man on supplementary benefit, who cannot claim Family Income Supplement because FIS payments are not made for part-time work below thirty hours a week. Nevertheless, it is also true, as we shall suggest below, that older family men receive less than their fair share of offers under CP.

The CP is also geographically imbalanced with London, the South-East and the Midlands having far fewer places than would be expected, given the scale of their long-term unemployment problems.[7] Within Cleveland County there is also an imperfect distribution of CP places with Hartlepool having a far greater share than would be justified by the number of its long-term unemployed, while Stockton and Langbaurgh are under-represented. Overall, then, CP scores only very imperfectly on our first criterion in that its targeting is not as well directed as it could be and that it is not reaching many of the most disadvantaged of the long-term unemployed.

There is no doubt that CP scores very highly on cost-effectiveness (criterion 2). The net cost per person off the unemployment register is estimated at only £2,050 in 1987−8,[8] making CP more than twenty times as cost-effective as income-tax cuts in reducing unemployment, which is a huge difference in magnitude. Indeed, one might note that the net cost of providing a place on the programme has fallen by 20 per cent since 1983−4.[9] 87 per cent of the costs of CP are labour costs and the average wage under the scheme has risen only half as fast as average earnings in the economy as a whole. Operating costs have been fixed at £440 per participant since the inception of the programme and have thus declined significantly in real terms.

In fact, this real decline in the already very meagre provision for operating costs goes a very long way in explaining why the MSC cannot provide any useful information about the social benefits to the wider community which the CP hopes to provide. Certainly many CP schemes are on the margins of usefulness although there are no actual examples of unemployed people digging holes and then filling them in again. Nevertheless, gardening, painting scout huts and other environmental work which makes up about one-third of CP activity do not appear to produce an enormously useful output. There are examples of imaginative use of labour, however. The South Tees Health Authority has organised a Dental Health Education Programme which uses CP participants in a scheme designed to raise standards of dental care amongst children in schools. There are also a number of national initiatives which are using CP labour for schemes of renovation in the inner cities and wider community refurbishment projects. The work organised by Neighbourhood Energy Action in insulating the homes of elderly people on supplementary benefit (see Chapter 11) appears to be especially useful. The MSC itself has recognised the need to increase the number of CPs which provide useful output and is trying to remedy the dearth of good information which would allow for a more detailed judgement on whether CP passes criterion 3. On present evidence the case is not proven.

CP work is easy to organise in a short space of time, so criterion 4 is clearly satisfied. For the moment we will pass over the issue of the impact of CP on inflation, precisely because in order to answer that question we must first look at whether CP raises the chances of participants finding permanent employment opportunities.

We have already stressed that CP is imperfectly targeted at the least disadvantaged of the long-term unemployed, that is to say that it indulges in 'creaming' by recruiting those people who have the best opportunity of finding work without the MSC's help. Table 7.4 illustrates that CP participants are more than twice as likely to have academic qualifications when compared with the long-term unemployed as a whole and more than four times as likely to hold technical qualifications. Two-thirds of the CP client group hold no qualifications, but only one quarter of participants. A 1984 survey of CP sponsors and managing agents revealed that only 4 per cent said that they accepted all who applied and there were about two unsuccessful applicants for each successful one.[10] CP sponsors admit themselves that they are often reluctant to hire people who have been out of work for a very long time, who appear demotivated, are older, or lack basic skills. The evidence suggests very strongly that CP employers, with few exceptions, repeat the same recruitment patterns as conventional employers (under the constraints imposed

Table 7.4   Reported Highest Qualifications of Community Programme
Participants (%)

	CP participants	CP client group
CSE (Excluding Grade 1)	13.0	7.4
'O' levels	24.0	11.3
'A' levels	7.0	2.7
Degree	5.0	2.0
Technical qualifications	24.0	5.8
No qualifications	25.0	65.0

by CP rules on eligibility) and largely by-pass the most intractable group
of long-term unemployed.

CP managers in Cleveland are often ex-BSC and ICI and as such bring
with them the same recruitment and work practices which have been
characteristic of British employers for years. Two-thirds of CP managers
and supervisors do not stay with CP for more than a year. Turnover
among MSC staff responsisble for the scrutiny and evaluation of CP is
also very high, with the consequence that few people have built up the
skills and long-term relations with CP managers that would allow them
to perform their task with complete confidence. Indeed, this constant
turnover of MSC staff is an all-pervasive problem as schemes are form-
ulated, expanded, changed in emphasis and at a tremendous pace, which
generates constant managerial headaches. MSC personnel recognise
themselves the limitations in what they are trying to do, as the first quote
at the beginning of this chapter, from the head of the MSC division in
Cleveland which is responsible for CP, recognises.[11] Indeed, the MSC's
own investigation into CP[12] stressed the intense pressure on its grass
roots staff, which might lead to a reformulation of MSC as 'Management Skills Under Crisis'.

Not only are the recruits to the CP not the most unskilled of the long-
term unemployed, but the CP itself offers little training. On-the-job training must be paid for out of normal operating costs or by reducing
participants' wages, and is usually narrowly confined to the work in hand,
health and safety procedures, and so on. In 1986–7 the MSC spent £5.7
million providing off-the-job training to 15,000 participants. Thus one
half of one per cent of the total CP budget was used to provide training
for about 6 per cent of CP participants. A plan to increase the number
of participants in receipt of training to 50,000 each year was vetoed in
1986 to save £15–20 million from the CP budget. The MSC has no

systematic evidence that CP-linked training raises the chances of participants finding jobs. The only survey which looked at this question suggested that training did significantly improve job prospects but the sample only covered 94 people so it is wise not to draw firm conclusions.[13]

The last follow-up survey of CP participants conducted in the summer of 1985 suggests that 28 per cent of leavers enter full or part-time employment and 65 per cent go back into unemployment.[14] Ten months after the survey, 35 per cent of participants were in employment and 50 per cent unemployed, with others in training or on other MSC schemes. In the north of England only 15 per cent of leavers found employment, compared with 77 per cent who left for unemployment. Women and participants aged under twenty-five do better in finding employment and of course this exactly mirrors the employment trends we outlined in Chapter 3, with the bias in recruitment in favour of women and the young and against older, very long-term unemployed men. The MSC has suggested that '. . . the statistical evidence on the extent to which CP improves participants' job prospects should be treated with caution.'[15] This of course is 'Whitehall speak' for saying that the case for CP under criterion 6 is also *not proven*.

Needless to say there is no information on the quality of jobs obtained by participants, the level of pay or level of skill involved, and whether any further training is provided. We have no idea whether the improved 'skills' or 'morale' which CP is supposed to impart to the long-term unemployed simply erode again very quickly if the participant returns to joblessness after a spell on the scheme. There is now anecdotal evidence of people working on CP, leaving for unemployment and then rejoining the scheme again after six or twelve months have elapsed. Thus CP is becoming not a scheme for rehabilitation of the long-term unemployed into the normal labour market, but a more permanent feature of that labour market, as the second quote at the beginning of the chapter suggests.

The MSC worries that CP does little to upgrade workers so that they may compete in more skilled labour markets.[16] This is not surprising, given that the work is usually part-time, very labour-intensive, and offers little training. This throws considerable doubt on the thesis that CP participants leave the scheme to join in the ranks of the short-term unemployed who are doing their 'bit' to hold down wage inflation. We mentioned in Chapter 1 the evidence that wage pressure is concentrated in the top half of the income-distribution range. However CP increases the competitive pressure in the already fiercely competitive markets for unskilled and semi-skilled labour. We have to leave entirely open the question of whether CP really does contribute to reintegrating the long-term unemployed into the labour market and make a significant contribution to countering the unbalanced recovery.

The rule that CP should not perform work which would otherwise be carried out within two years is designed expressly to prevent the substitution of CP for the normal activities of local authorities and voluntary bodies. The formal evidence presented by the MSC argues that substitution is indeed kept to about 4 per cent,[17] although anecdotal evidence would suggest that this is an underestimate. Nevertheless, we will leave the benefit of the doubt with the MSC. However, the Commission's own analysis of CP notes the paradox that the two-year rule logically implies that CP can only perform work of marginal social value so that the outputs from CP are automatically limited.[18] The attempt to make cost-effectiveness the key criterion for judging the scheme also limits its usefulness. Low pay levels imply part-time work and the exclusion of family men, while low operating costs make the work necessarily labour-intensive and such as to involve very little training, which in turn limits the value of the scheme in rehabilitating the long-term unemployed.

This, then, is the thundering paradox of CP — if costs are to be kept low and substitution avoided, the scheme can only perform work of marginal social value and cannot offer the patterns of work and training which will allow participants to compete more effectively in the labour market. But if you raise the quality of work and training and begin to produce output which is of greater social value, you will not only raise costs significantly but automatically begin to substitute for work which is already being done.

This paradox is explicitly noted by the authors of the MSC's own report on CP who argue that '... if the aim is a high productivity, high efficiency scheme, then what is needed is a different programme with different objectives.'[19] To put it another way: the CP cannot hope to satisfy simultaneously all of our criteria. If you emphasise cost-effectiveness alone (criterion 2) you sacrifice all of the outputs of the programme (criteria 3, 5 and 6). If you emphasise the outputs as paramount, then you must accept more expense *and* the MSC becomes the inappropriate administrative body because it cannot prevent substitution. Indeed, a 'high-quality CP' becomes indistinguishable from normal public-sector employment *except* that the jobs only last for one year.

The limited duration of the CP creates another set of debilitating problems. The evidence suggests that work effort and morale begin to decline after about nine months on CP as the participant begins to contemplate a return to unemployment.[20] Moreover, any skills which have been learnt are often simply lost again. About one-third of CP places is in the social services, either with voluntary agencies or with the local authorities. In caring for elderly, disabled or mentally handicapped people it is very important to build up long-term client relationships, for these vulnerable people cannot be passed from person to person without, in many cases, serious adverse consequences. But CP workers spend some months building up a relationship with a client and are then replaced, to their disadvantage and often to the great distress of the individual for whom they have been caring.

Suppose that the MSC receives proposals to fund one project caring for some elderly people, another targeted at the mentally handicapped, and a third at disadvantaged young people, but only has enough money for two projects. How does it rank the three projects? Who should receive priority? Is a labour board in a position to make these decisions? Do MSC staff have the knowledge and skills to decide a whole range of priorities for social policy, for investment in the infrastructure and for the environment as well as for education and, in addition, perform its function as a labour board, or is the MSC being asked to do too much work? The MSC staff in Cleveland responsible for CP work in the social services sector recognised their lack of expertise and evolved an *ad hoc* arrangement with the County Social Services Department by which they had to approve any proposed funding for a voluntary body working in the social field.[21] Even this arrangement has not prevented overlap, duplication and confusion in the provision of social services in Cleveland. Moreover, the constant turnover in MSC staff means that the social services have to renegotiate the arrangement whenever the individual responsible for this part of CP is replaced.

In Chapter 11 we intend to develop the thesis that, if we want a high-quality programme which does work of greater social value but avoids substitution, preserves long-run client relations and allows for a sensible allocation of resources in accordance with well-thought-out priorities, *then the MSC is not the right administrative agency.* This follows from the paradoxes inherent in CP and the overstretching of the MSC's management resources. Perhaps the MSC would do better if it concentrated on being a labour board, rather than being forced to be all things to all men.

Postscript

In November 1987 the government decided to merge the Community Programme with the Job Training Scheme and elements of the Adult Training Strategy (see Chapter 12), in order to offer a unified programme which will aim to provide, by Autumn 1988, 600,000 places for one year to people who have been out of work for over six months. The programme will offer flexible modules of work experience, intensive training and education, and will be full-time. It does therefore address some of the problems discussed above and follows some of the proposals for reform outlined in Chapter 12.

Participants are to be paid the equivalent of their benefits, plus a premium of more than £5 per week, to cover expenses. It is unclear whether this premium will be generous enough to encourage participation, or whether the programme will suffer from the recruiting difficulties experienced by the Job Training Scheme (Chapter 12). The government plans to spend £1,500 million to provide 600,000 places. The present CP costs £1,000 million for 250,000 places. The government must be assuming that it can cut the costs per participant on the new programme by over one-third. Given this, how can it offer enhanced training, make the scheme full-time, and pay a premium generous enough to encourage long-term unemployed family men to participate? We can re-emphasise the paradox of CP: if you want to raise the outputs of the programme you must accept greater expense. Moreover, the two-year rule will remain, so that the programme will still only be able to fund projects of marginal social value. It is not clear whether, or how, the new programme will succeed in boosting private-sector involvement, which is negligible in CP, and the local authorities and voluntary agencies are very unhappy about the benefits-plus payments formula. Once again the MSC's organisation is going to be turned upside down.

Notes

1. Mr Geoff Garnett, Head of the Employment and Enterprise Group of the MSC in Cleveland, responsible for administering the Community Programme; quoted in *The Financial Times*, 7 April 1987. Mr Garnett was a useful source of information for the author.
2. Unemployed worker quoted on p. 60 of Robinson (1987).
3. Jackman *et al.* (1986) contains an accessible discussion of flows into and out of the labour market.

4. These figures are from *Hansard*, 26 January 1987. See also the article on Job Clubs in the Spring 1987 issue of the *Unemployment Bulletin* published by the Unemployment Unit.

5. 'Creaming' on MSC schemes is exactly analogous to 'creaming' by schools. One cannot compare an independent school, which creams off the best children, with a state comprehensive school, which must accept all comers, unless one controls for differences in pupil intake.

6. The effect of the low wage in deterring family men is stressed in the official MSC report on CP, Normington *et al.* (1986). In 1987 a proposal was put forward to pay CP participants the equivalent of their supplementary benefit plus £16 as a way of removing the deterrent to family men. This might be a stop-gap prior to a more fundamental reform of the entire tax and benefits system as it relates to families on low pay.

7. See Normington *et al.* (1986), p. 25.

8. Public Expenditure White Paper, January 1987.

9. Normington *et al.* (1986), p. 11.

10. Normington *et al.* (1986), p. 32.

11. See note 1. It should be emphasised that most local MSC staff are very helpful to outside investigators. The official MSC report, Normington *et al.* (1986), is notable for its honest and candid self-criticism with respect to the operation of CP. But how many politicians or journalists who talk about MSC schemes have actually read the report in depth?

12. Normington *et al.* (1986), p. 5 of the 'Summary of Main Findings' and p. 68 of the main report.

13. Normington *et al.* (1986), p. 45.

14. The results of this survey were published in the MSC quarterly Report, June 1986.

15. Normington *et al.* (1986), p. 2 of the 'Summary of Main Findings' and p. 37 of the main report.

16. Normington *et al.* (1986), p. 38.

17. Normington *et al.* (1986), p. 24.

18. Normington *et al.* (1986), p. 9.

19. Normington *et al.* (1986), p. 9. It is not clear that many writers in this area have grasped the implications of this paradox. Jackman *et al.* (1986) clearly has not.

20. This was stressed by the CP managing agents in conversations with the author.

21. The author's conversation with Michael Bishop of Cleveland Social Services Department. Normington *et al.* (1986), p. 46, also noted the poor integration of normal local authority work with CP projects.

8

Lessons From Other Places

'It's not that we don't ever learn lessons from the experience of other countries, but that usually we learn precisely the wrong lessons.'[1]

Britain is not an island in anything except the true geographical sense of the word. The fortunes of the British economy are intimately bound up with the fortunes of the rest of the world. It must also be true that we could learn lessons from the experience of other countries, many of whom have done much better than Britain in the last twenty years. It is an important reminder to those people who believe that an unemployment rate of 10 per cent or more is inevitable, that the unemployment rates of Japan and Sweden have never risen above 3 per cent in recent times, and that the rate in the United States plunged from over 10 per cent in 1983 to less than 6 per cent in 1987. However, to note these statistics is not enough: it also helps to understand clearly why other countries have performed better and to resist the temptation to accept glib clichés.

The two countries we are going to investigate in some detail are Sweden and the United States. The comparison is most interesting because these two countries appear at first sight to represent the extremes in the Western World: the 'capitalist, free market' model and the 'socialist, welfare state' model. If we refer back to the tables in Chapter 1, we can see that Sweden has been especially successful in maintaining very low unemployment, although its record on inflation is less good. The United States had higher unemployment than the average for the whole of Europe for about thirty years, until 1983; then US unemployment came down sharply while European unemployment continued to creep up. This warrants a note of caution: any theory which seeks to explain America's recent comparatively good performance must also explain why America performed so poorly during the previous thirty years. To rely solely on certain fixed attributes of US society, such as alleged greater mobility or a reputation for enterprise, in order to explain a very recent fall in unemployment relative to Europe, is not convincing if we look at the post-war period as a whole. Another interesting point to note is that Sweden and the United States (along with Canada) have had rather poor productivity growth in recent decades. The tremendous affluence of these countries is in part a function of past success, before 1950, rather than post-war performance, when other countries (but not Britain) registered much faster growth and thus began to catch up with North America and Scandinavia.

Perhaps the most interesting comparison to be made between Sweden and the United States is that both countries have exactly the same number of long-term unemployed people as a proportion of total unemployment (Table 1.2). Only about one in eight of their unemployed had been out of work for over a year in 1984 compared with two out of five in Britain.[2] Given the theme of this book and its focus upon long-term unemployment, it is this comparison on which we intend to concentrate in the next few pages, as well as some other lessons which we might learn from the experience of the United States. In particular we want to draw some lessons from the experience of labour-market programmes in the two countries.

Considerable interest has been generated in Britain recently over the alleged lessons to be learned from the American 'workfare' programme. This has been presented as the idea that unemployed people in receipt of welfare benefits should be required to 'work off' their benefits in some form of job or training placement. In practice it means making the programmes of the Manpower Services Commission, which we looked at in the last chapter and will take up again in Chapter 12, *mandatory* in that anyone who does not take a place on a scheme will lose all rights to unemployment or supplementary benefit. Some observers have suggested that the Job Training Scheme (Chapter 12) has elements of the workfare ideology in it. Participants receive only the equivalent of their supplementary benefit on the scheme (renamed a 'training allowance') and may face sanctions if they are reluctant to take up a place. So what are the true lessons of workfare as applied in the USA?

The first thing to note is that within the United States there are two fundamentally different philosophical approaches to what workfare is supposed to achieve. The first argument is that over-generous welfare benefits are the root cause of much of the unemployment in the USA because they discourage people from taking a job. Workfare is seen as a way of forcing those people off benefit and back into work who can reasonably be expected to hold down a job. The second argument is completely different in that it suggests that the main reason people become dependent on welfare is because they lack the education, skills and supporting services (such as child care facilities), which would allow them a fair opportunity to compete for whatever suitable jobs are available, recognising that suitable jobs are themselves in short supply. Workfare is seen as a way of providing education, training and careful work placement so that people can build up the skills and confidence to rejoin the labour market.

In Britain one can detect exactly the same division of opinion between those who blame the long-term unemployed for finding life on the dole too easy and those who blame the institutions in Britain for failing to help the long-term unemployed compete fairly in the jobs market. The key argument of the first group is that we have to find ways of making the long-term unemployed take very low-paid jobs by threatening withdrawal of benefits, because the unemployment problem is seen to be a function of an over-generous welfare state and a blockage in the lower half of the labour market.[3] Implicitly, these critics would like to replace our sixth criterion for judging employment programmes (which stresses their rehabilitative role) with 'To what extent will this programme lower expectations of participants so that they will accept very low-paid and low-skilled jobs?' The keenest advocate of applying workfare principles in Britain sees the main advantages from workfare following on from an equivalent 30 per cent cut in welfare benefits available to the unemployed who do not want a place on the programme.[4]

The evidence which we presented in Chapters 3 and 4 suggested strongly that it is very unfair to blame the unemployed or the welfare state for their being out of work. The unemployed are by no means unrealistic in their expectations and are already prepared to accept jobs at low pay and using skills which are at or below existing levels. There is scanty evidence that any more than a tiny minority of the unemployed prefer dependence on benefits and no rational way of blaming the upsurge in unemployment since 1979 on a benefits system which has become significantly less generous over this period. The more convincing evidence suggests that the supplementary benefits system does not provide a fully adequate income for the long-term unemployed, many of whom are at serious risk from poverty. To the extent that there is a prob-

lem with the labour market and a threat of a resurgence in wage inflation, the problem lies in the top half of the income distribution range
and the MSC schemes are not contributing to reducing this pressure.
We can find no evidence, then, to jettison our sixth criterion for the alternative suggested above.

It is also surprising to discover that there are very few real lessons
to be learnt from the actual experience of workfare programmes in the
United States. This follows from an obvious but frequently overlooked
fact. In the United States only about half the unemployed receive any
form of public financial assistance. The issue of working off their benefits
hardly arises because many of them receive absolutely no benefits in
the first place! Workfare provisions apply to adult members of households
which are in receipt of Aid-To-Families with Dependent Children
(AFDC). In 1983, 93 per cent of AFDC families were headed by women
(divorced, unmarried or abandoned)[5] and most of these were exempt
from workfare because they had children who were below school age.
In most states, workfare is targeted at women with children of school
age who are not disqualified because of ill health or disability and at
the small number of two-parent families with an unemployed but
employable father. Thus workfare, as *practised* in the United States, is
actually largely irrelevant to our problem of large-scale, mainly male,
long-term unemployment.

It is hard to prove conclusively that the actual practice of workfare
delivers benefits on the basis of our sixth criterion. This is because there
have been few very carefully controlled studies of the effects of workfare
programmes in rehabilitating 'welfare mothers', which have allowed for
the impact of our old friends, 'creaming', 'deadweight' and 'substitution'. What evidence is available suggests that the job-search, training
and work-placement schemes which are available under the workfare
provisions in various states are most often targeted at the most employable
people on the welfare rolls and by-pass the harder-to-place recipients
who have been dependent on welfare for a very long time. It is therefore
unclear whether anybody is finding work because of the programme or
because they would have found work anyway. Also, we cannot be sure
that those people who may find jobs because of workfare are not simply
displacing other, less fortunate, people and in particular the millions of
men who are not entitled to benefit or any other kind of help. The US
General Accounting Office (GAO) could find no conclusive evidence
that workfare was fulfilling any of our six criteria and in particular there

was little evidence that the programmes helped AFDC recipients find
permanent employment.[6] The GAO also made the same set of criticisms
of workfare which we applied to CP: inadequate attention to education
and training, marginal social benefit from the work schemes and inadequate staffing in the organisations responsible for managing and
evaluating the programmes.

Thus there really is very little to learn from America's workfare. How
has Sweden managed to keep its long-term unemployment so low? Some
commentators have argued that it is Sweden's imaginative labour market
policies which are to be congratulated and which ought to be emulated
here in Britain. Certainly Sweden has a long history of active intervention in the labour market dating back to the inter-war period and the
number of people participating in various employment and training
measures has increased from about 3½ per cent of the labour force in
1979 to 5 per cent today.[7] There are in fact similarities between these
programmes and the schemes operated by the MSC in this country. About
20 per cent of the places are in temporary jobs, mainly with the local
authorities, and are not unlike CP placements. Youth and training
measures cover 2 per cent of the labour force and are akin to the YTS
and JTS in this country. Many disabled people are catered for by sheltered
work schemes which in Britain are covered by the requirement that all
employers with more than twenty workers should employ a quota of 3
per cent disabled people (though only one-third of employers actually
comply).

If we exclude sheltered work, about 3 per cent of Sweden's labour
force are in special employment and training schemes. In Chapter 7 we
discovered that, in 1987−8, about 900,000 British people should be participating in similar MSC schemes and this is about 3½ per cent of the
British labour force! In other words, the scale of the existing British
labour market policies is just about equivalent to the numbers in Sweden.
This simple arithmetic suggests that it cannot be Sweden's own labour
market schemes which alone account for Sweden's impressive unemployment record. It should also be stressed that there has been no recent and
detailed attempt to see whether these schemes fulfill any of our criteria
and, in particular, whether the programmes have improved participants'
permanent employment prospects.[8]

So how then do we explain Sweden's record? We have suggested that
the single most important reason for the explosion in British unemployment in the early 1980s was the sharp over-valuation of the pound which
put British firms under intense competitive pressure and led to massive

labour shedding. To the extent that there has been an economic recovery since 1983 it owes much to the reversal of the policy of maintaining a tight exchange rate. Sweden has followed an entirely different strategy involving a 16 per cent devaluation of the Swedish Krona in 1982−3. To put it another way, Sweden has never set out on an all-or-nothing policy of reducing inflation no matter what the consequences. It might also be argued that Sweden has something more than half an instrument in its centralised incomes policy, which has prevented any explosion in wages even if it has not given Sweden the very best of records on inflation and has come under recent strain.

Overall, one cannot help concluding that Sweden is a case study in how prevention is always better than cure and that it is wise not to allow an explosion in unemployment in the very first place. This limits what we can learn from Sweden, except that we should try to avoid going through the trauma of 1979−83 ever again. Sweden in fact is one country which has fulfilled the dream of William Beveridge in relying on the intelligent use of a wide range of instruments (monetary and fiscal, wage controls and labour market intervention) to prevent any serious unemployment from occurring, so that the issue of paying benefits to people out of work for a very long time hardly ever arises. Sweden does not face the problem of an unbalanced recovery which is by-passing the long-term unemployed because it has ensured that long-term unemployment is avoided as a major problem to begin with.

Sweden is one of only five countries (Austria, Norway, Switzerland and Japan being the others) which have contained unemployment at low levels. There are few obvious similarities between these countries. Switzerland's good performance has relied mainly on the expulsion of foreign guest workers as a means of reducing the labour force in bad times. The other four countries all have workable 'consensus'-based incomes policies and use subsidies, retraining and employment insurance schemes as instruments to prevent unemployment from getting out of hand in the first place. Nevertheless the differences between these countries are greater than the similarities, indicating that there must be more than one route to full employment.[9]

One very interesting characteristic of the Swedish economy is the very great strength of its private-sector companies; Volvo, Saab and Electrolux are all leaders in their fields. Sweden has the largest number of industrial robots per head of population in the world and its firms invest a consistently high proportion of profits in new technology and in the skills training which allows its workforce to adapt to changes in the world environment. This highlights the general point that it is quite possible to have a very competitive private sector in co-existence with a generous welfare state and high levels of personal taxation.[10] Efficiency and equality are not always, or even often, in conflict. The United States is more often declared the epitome of triumphant private enterprise. Certainly the present government's approach to regional and urban policies seems to draw upon experience in the United States which is supposed to prove the superiority of harnessing the private sector rather than relying on state intervention. Much of the urban programme in Britain is supposed to draw on US initiatives, but has the government really been learning the right lessons or some distorted ones?

The cities of the North-Eastern United States have seen something of the major changes in industrial structure and comparative advantage which have affected the major conurbations in Britain. Yet the economies of cities such as Pittsburgh and Baltimore and the state of Massachusetts have in recent years undergone a veritable transformation and a renaissance. The first correct lesson to learn is never to write off any city or region completely.

Massachusetts is the first interesting example. New England had for many years been overly dependent on its clothing and footwear industries which were under increasing competitive pressure from cheaper output produced in the southern states and abroad. Nevertheless, the industry has clawed its way back, mainly by emphasising high quality and investment in new technology and skills. This suggests that hard-hit industries can adapt, given time, and should not be written off any more than a whole region. Another interesting point to note is that Massachusetts is one of the largest recipients of Federal Defence and Space-related contracts (in relation to its population) of any state in the USA. It also has the largest concentration of educational institutions probably anywhere in the world. This makes the obvious point that the state's booming hi-tech economy has as much to do with government expenditure as private enterprise.[11]

If we remember this lesson and think about Britain, we might note that the three largest universities in the country are all in the South-East, as are about half of all private research and development institutions and that about two-thirds of all Ministry of Defence contracts go to firms in the region.[12] So is the prosperity of the South-East any the less to do with state spending than the prosperity of Massachusetts? And if Cleveland County had a big, fat, well-funded university and were the recipient of numerous defence contracts, might it not be prosperous too?

The more general point to be made is that we have only a very limited idea of the precise regional impact of government expenditure in Britain, so that it is unclear whether the relative prosperity of any part of the country is a function of private enterprise, state spending or, more likely, a combination of both. The amount of public money devoted to urban and regional policy is dwarfed by the implications of state activity as a whole for individual cities and regions.

The experience of Baltimore and Pittsburgh has been used as a blueprint by government for its programme of urban development grants (UDGs), urban regeneration grants (URGs) and the urban development corporations (UDCs) (see Chapter 6). The grants are directly modelled on the Urban Development Action Grant programme instituted in the USA in 1977. Under the UDG programme, local authorities in Britain can receive a 75 per cent subsidy from central government for joint development projects agreed with the private sector. Unfortunately, the UDG budget has been underspent, reflecting the constraints under which local authorities are being forced to operate, to the extent that they cannot even afford their 25 per cent share.[13] As we have noted in Chapter 6 the UDCs aim to by-pass the local authorities entirely by imposing central government control. This is based on a complete misrepresentation of the American example, where the leadership in urban regeneration has been provided by entrepreneurial *local* government. It is precisely because the *city* authorities in Baltimore and Pittsburgh have been given the leeway to do what they want in cooperation with the private sector that the momentum for change has been built up. It has had little to do with the federal government in Washington.

This brings us to a more general point: that at the moment Whitehall is trying to do everything itself and is constraining local authorities from making any contribution to tackling the economic problems of the communities of which they, not Whitehall, are supposed to be the democratic representatives. State intervention is bad if it is carried out by a local authority, but good if it is carried out by Whitehall. The result is the stifling of grass-roots initiative, which forms the basis for the argument in the next chapter.

Notes

1. An old LSE joke!
2. It should be noted that the US survey method of compiling unemployment

statistics is likely to lead to downward bias in the reported number of long-term unemployed people.

3. This is the line taken in Burton (1987).
4. Burton (1987).
5. Burghes (1987), p. 5. This excellent survey is the basis for many of the facts presented in this chapter.
6. The GAO report is reviewed in Burghes (1987), p. 12. The GAO is equivalent to the British National Audit Office (NAO) which is responsible for reviewing the MSC.
7. Jackman *et al.* (1986) contains an interesting discussion of Sweden's programmes and is the source of much of the information presented here.
8. This is accepted by Richard Jackman in his survey written for the 'Charter For Jobs Economic Report', No. 9, August/September 1986.
9. Further comparison of these countries is contained in Therbörn (1986). These countries are able to offer some form of job guarantee, but only from the starting point of very low unemployment.
10. See Bosworth and Rivlin (1987). Internationally, there is absolutely no correlation between the size of the public sector and a country's macroeconomic performance.
11. I owe this observation to David Storey.
12. See the article by Peter Marsh, 'The lure of the silicon glen', in *The Financial Times*, 12 November 1986. See also Chapter 11 in Armstrong and Taylor (1985).
13. Government ministers have suggested that the low take-up of UDGs is a function of the hostility of Labour local authorities to cooperation with the private sector. There is very little evidence other than the anecdotal for this. The Department of the Environment has been criticised for taking six months or more to process UDG applications.

9

The Response of the Grass Roots

'... trying to drain an ocean with a teaspoon.'[1]

In Chapter 2 we emphasised the dominance of Cleveland by three industries and two firms and suggested that the concentration of employment in large manufacturing establishments had made the county vulnerable to labour shedding and plant closure and made it harder for new small firms to prosper. Traditional regional policy has been downgraded and replaced by the alphabet agencies and by the government's 'Enterprise Strategy' designed to foster a rapid rate of growth of new firms and a resurgence of the entrepreneurial spirit. We have also witnessed a growth in recent years in grass roots initiatives — the progammes and activities of local authorities and a huge range of bodies which have been set up to foster the new spirit of enterprise.

The northern region of England has fewer people in self-employment and one of the lowest rates of new firm formation in the United Kingdom.[2] This is *not* simply a function of the industrial structure of the region with its emphasis on very capital-intensive manufacturing.[3] It would appear to be the case that, even when we control for this bias, the propensity to enter self-employment in the North is still significantly below the national average. There is a tendency amongst some researchers to resort to emphasising unspecified 'cultural' differences as an explanation for the apparent lack of 'enterprise' in a place like Cleveland. In fact it would be worth stressing that we still remain a little ignorant as to why certain regions (or countries) have a consistently superior performance in generating new firms. Nevertheless, we can make some germane points. In the last chapter we noted that the South-East has the largest concentration of both public and private research establishments, universities and firms in receipt of defence contracts; and the South-East has as its centre London, which is the hub of business intelligence. This pattern is heavily related to the impact of public expenditure and is a reminder that we should treat with caution explanations which rely on pointing to private enterprise as the only explanatory variable.

The most convincing author in this field has pioneered an index of entrepreneurship by region (Table 9.1) which is obtained by averaging the rank position of each region in a number of factors which are thought to significantly affect the rate of new firm formation.[4] It can be seen that the northern region is bottom and, unsurprisingly, the South-East is top. If we look at the factors contained in the index, an entrepreneurial region is one which has an existing concentration of small- or medium-sized firms and a high proportion of well-educated people, including those with previous experience of managing a small firm and expertise in a particular market, with access to capital, often through owning a house. Conversely, a less entrepreneurial region is likely to have an overhang of big manufacturing plants, a large number of manual workers and proportionately fewer people with higher education and with access to capital more limited. To put it succinctly, the typical, successful entrepreneur is likely to be middle-class, well-educated, with managerial or technical skills; a home owner who has previously worked in another small or medium-sized firm in the same industry and in a prospering region where risk is minimised. The typical, successful entrepreneur is *not* a redundant steel worker with little managerial knowledge and obsolescent skills, still less a school leaver with no experience and no capital.[5]

Table 9.1 Index of Entrepreneurship by Region

Region	Entrepreneurship Index
South-East	9.2
South-West	7.6
East Anglia	6.9
North-West	6.6
East Midlands	6.1
West Midlands	5.3
Scotland	5.1
Yorkshire/Humberside	4.6
Northern Ireland	4.4
Wales	3.7
North	3.5

This strongly suggests that the whole process is cumulative, in that a prosperous region with an existing structure of successful small firms and skilled people will spin off more small firms to employ more skilled people and so further enhance prosperity. Cleveland appears to be locked into an alternative vicious circle in that the large branch plants shed labour and depress the local economy, without generating the relevant skills which would encourage the creation of new firms.

Thus at first sight the government's enterprise strategy, with its emphasis on small business creation, seems correctly targeted. Moreover, it is alleged that there are straws in the wind which suggest that the North is improving its relative position, as the proportion of people in self-employment seems to be rising at a faster rate in the North than in Britain as a whole.[6] Are we therefore witnessing a resurgence of enterprise, which the government could claim is a function of the success of its policies? In Chapter 3 we noted that self-employment has been a significant source of the growth in jobs since 1983, but if we look more closely at the actual dynamics of employment change the picture is less encouraging. There has been an enormous growth in the sub-contracting of peripheral functions such as maintenance and cleaning by large companies hell-bent on reducing their direct labour costs. To give a specific example: BSC contracts out maintenance at its Teesside plants and is able to reduce its workforce by 1,000 as a result. Half of the redundant workers are re-employed in various small businesses, performing exactly the same function which they previously performed as direct employees of the corporation. Employment in large *manufacturing* firms falls by 1,000, but appears to be partly compensated for by an increase of 500 in employment in small *service* businesses. The increase in employment in small firms is directly *caused* by the contraction in large firms and is not an example of entrepreneurial resurgence, but is a function of the recession and the lessons it has taught management about keeping a lean employment structure.[7]

Could the formation of new small businesses hope to compensate fully for labour shedding in the large manufacturing firms? From what we know about the dynamics of small business growth the answer is 'no'.[8] To replace the 16,000 redundancies in BSC on Teesside since 1976 would require the creation of between two and two-and-a-half thousand new businesses in the county, of which nearly 1,500 would not survive anyway (and half of these would fail within two or three years) and less than twenty would be employing more than one hundred people within a decade. This remorseless arithmetic suggests that even if new firm for-

mation rates in Cleveland *could* be raised to the national average, new
businesses on their own could not hope to compensate for massive labour
shedding in existing firms.

However, government strategy also suffers from being biased towards
those regions which already have a large number of small firms. Since
1979 more than one hundred measures have been introduced in Britain
which are specifically aimed at small firms, at an estimated cost to the
Exchequer of about £500 million in 1983.[9] This confusing plethora of
subsidies and initiatives suggests that state intervention is only bad when
Labour governments aim it at large firms, but is acceptable when aimed
by Conservative ministers at small businesses. None of these subsidies
is aimed regionally — rather, they are indiscriminately available to any
small firm in the country. The index of regional entrepreneurship (Table
9.1) seems to have predicted very accurately which regions benefit most
from these subsidies, and of course they are the regions with an existing
concentration of small firms.[10] What limited evidence we have suggests
that small businesses steer their recruitment heavily towards labour
market entrants (young people and married women). The government's
enterprise strategy thus completely fails our first criterion for judging
employment programmes in that it is acting to reinforce the regional imbalance in the economic recovery and is largely by-passing the long-
term unemployed.

Rather than try to evaluate in detail this morass of subsidies we intend
to concentrate on the Enterprise Allowance Scheme (EAS) administered
by the Manpower Services Commission, which offers a payment of £40
per week for one year to any unemployed person in receipt of benefit
who has £1,000 of capital to invest in his/her proposed new business.
Nearly half of those who claim the allowance will have been unemployed
for under six months and only just over one quarter will have been out
of work for more than a year.[11] Fewer older people claim the allowance
and family men are excluded because of course the £40 allowance is
far too small an income to support a wife and children. Thus, once again,
this scheme is tending to help the least disadvantaged of the unemployed
while by-passing the older family men who have been out of work for
some time. As one would expect, take-up of the EAS varies regionally,
with Cleveland having one of the lowest rates. This is partly explained
by the fact that few of the unemployed people in the county have access
to even £1,000 in capital. The EAS thus aggravates the existing regional
imbalances in employment growth.

The MSC estimates that up to half of the participants in the EAS would have gone into self-employment anyway (so this constitutes 'deadweight'). The MSC has no direct evidence on whether EAS-supported businesses are merely displacing people employed in other businesses; but 60 per cent of EAS participants admit that they employ a strategy of undercutting rivals. Most businesses are set up in services such as retailing or hairdressing, where demand is limited by the extent of local prosperity, so that displacement of existing businesses is likely to be very high. In fact, most EAS businesses are operating on the margins of economic activity, dependent on the relative prosperity of their local economy and limited often by their owners' unwillingness to expand and take on other workers, with the implied loss of personal control. Taking into account MSC estimates of deadweight and displacement, the net cost of the EAS is said to be £1,800 per person taken off the unemployment register.[12] The scheme is cost-effective to be sure, but it is not clear that it satisfies any of our other criteria in that it is imperfectly targeted and, given the marginality of the businesses, does not seem to offer significant wider benefits.

Out of every 100 EAS businesses, 13 fold within a year and another 34 do not survive beyond three years. Of the 53 survivors, more than 60 per cent will have no other employees, and only two or three will be employing more than half a dozen people. For every 100 entrants, 105 new jobs will have been created (the 53 original survivors and 52 people employed by them, half part-time), but only 5 per cent of the survivors will be employing nearly half the people. This stresses a point which has already been made with respect to non-EAS-supported businesses, that ' . . . the performance of small firms is extremely diverse. Significant job creation takes place in very few small firms.'[13] EAS-supported businesses are significantly less likely to survive (only 53 per cent survive three years as opposed to 70 per cent of ordinary new businesses) and significantly less likely to provide additional employment.

The MSC itself has recognised the importance of boosting both the survival rate of EAS businesses and their ability to generate jobs for other people. The first thing to note is that the MSC applies *no* test of the viability of a business proposal before agreeing to pay the allowance and only 4 per cent of applicants are rejected. Beyond an initial one-day seminar, no training is offered and there is only a very limited follow-up service. Only 40 per cent of participants obtain assistance from an advisory body such as an enterprise agency. In Cleveland the participant would have at least eighteen different bodies to turn to (Table 9.2). When we consider this confusion and overlap in the provision of suppor-

Table 9.2   Bodies in Cleveland Providing 'Enterprise' Advice

British Steel Corporation (Industry)
Cleveland Co-operative Agency
Cleveland County Council
Cleveland Enterprise Agency
Cleveland Youth Business Centre
Council for Small Industries in Rural Areas
Durham University Business School/Enterprise North
English Estates
Hartlepool New Development Support Limited
Hartlepool Enterprise Agency
All 4 Borough Councils
Small Firms Service, Department of Employment
Teesside and District Chamber of Commerce
Teesside Polytechnic — Department of Management and Centre for
                              Industry/Education Liaison
Teesside Small Business Club

tive services to small businesses along with the one hundred or more state initiatives designed to aid small firms, we can see why some businessmen complain that the present system is nothing short of a chaotic mess.

If we look at the type of EAS business which is most likely to survive, we find that those participants who would have set up without the allowance and who intended from the start to invest more than the minimum £1,000 are significantly less likely to fail, but that businesses set up by people under 30 and by women have a significantly lower survival rate.[14] The one in eight participants who start a manufacturing enterprise are no less likely to fail, but if they do succeed are significantly more likely to take on additional full-time employees. Such enterprises are also more likely to grow to a point where they may begin to displace imports or even begin exporting themselves and so contribute to our trading performance.

The 'social entrepreneurs'[15] who run the network of over 300 local enterprise agencies which have sprung up since the recession are adamant that most of the reasons for early business failure are avoidable. These agencies are staffed by secondees from big local employers (half of the Cleveland Enterprise Agency staff comes from ICI). The cynics might comment that such employers are merely salvaging their consciences by providing this kind of help, and that it allows them to claim that they are paying attention to the social consequences of employment change so that that change is made more palatable. More cogent criticism would reflect that firms like ICI are very much in a minority in taking these kinds of initiatives seriously and the trade unions are noticeable by their almost complete absence from these efforts designed to create new jobs. Indeed it should be noted that some firms and some unions are positively hostile to new businesses because they are perceived as competitive threats.

Internationally, it might be noted that there is no significant correlation between the proportion of employment in small firms or the number of people who are self-employed and a country's unemployment performance.[16] If we refer back to Table 1.2 we can note that Japan and Sweden have had the lowest unemployment rates over the last two decades. Japan has the highest proportion of employment in small firms in the OECD and one of the highest rates of self-employment, while Sweden has significantly fewer small firms and the lowest rate of self-employment of any OECD country. Italy and Britain have the worst unemployment performances. Italy has the highest rate of self-employment in the OECD and a quite significant small firms sector, while Britain has a less important small firms sector and an average rate of self-employment. Overall there appears to be no obvious and consistent pattern which would allow one to say that a well-functioning economy must have lots of small firms and self-employed people.

Indeed, when people talk about a resurgence of enterprise, it is not at all clear what they mean or whether they have grasped the right nettle. We observed in Chapter 1 that most research has suggested that the long-run problems of the British economy include a poor record of investment in education and training, inattention to consensual industrial relations and a lack of competitive pressure. British firms are not 'enterprising' enough in the sense that they consistently neglect skills training and the development of productive relations with their workforce. The solution to this lack of 'enterprise' lies in desirable reforms within *existing* firms rather than simply the creation of a great many new ones.

The emphasis of the local enterprise agencies is beginning to focus on developing the skills which are necessary to identify those four or five businesses out of every one hundred start-ups which are going to grow quite quickly into significant employers, producing an output which can be traded internationally. There is in fact a consistent set of indicators which can be used to identify these potential success stories.[17] Towards the beginning of the chapter we described the kind of individual who is most likely to be a successful entrepreneur. At some stage he is going to run into problems such as lack of capital or skilled labour or difficulties in obtaining access to overseas markets, and it is at this point that help from an enterprise agency or a public body can make a significant difference. Existing government strategy has not recognised that it is the *quality* of small and growing firms which matters, not the quantity of new firms which spring up. Likewise, left-wing critics must recognise that there is no overall lack of capital in the British economy, but rather it is the quality of skills in directing that capital to the firms that can generate the most employment which is deficient. Rather than create a new set of national or regional institutions, industrial policy should try to build on the existing grass-roots network of local agencies as the conduit for channelling help to growing enterprises.

We can outline what this would mean for Cleveland. There is a pressing need to rationalise both the programmes of assistance and the bodies through which this assistance is channelled. The MSC should insist on a business plan to be vetted by a local enterprise agency before paying an enterprise allowance. The MSC should contract out advisory and evaluation services for small businesses to, at most, one or two agencies which in turn could draw on more specialised bodies for specific help. The small businessmen must have only one or two points of entry if the system is not to generate hopeless confusion. Agencies should not be afraid to turn people down if their planned business is clearly unsound. This is much kinder than encouraging an individual to risk £1,000 of his own capital on a worthless venture. The agencies would concentrate on identifying the growing firms and channelling a comprehensive package of assistance to them, but before we outline precisely what we have in mind here, it is important that we look at other examples of recent grass-roots initiatives — the programmes of the local authorities.

> ... public sector finance is a minefield (and in the case of local government finance it seems that more mines are being laid every month).[18]

Britain in the 1980s has been characterised by a state of open warfare between central and local government, motivated by the desire of Whitehall to curb the alleged excesses and inefficiencies of a number of left-wing councils. In 1983 the government set up the Audit Commission as an independent body charged with achieving value for money in local government. It would appear to be the case that one of the main tactics in this Whitehall—Townhall civil war is the art of selective reading. Government ministers only read those sections of Audit Commission reports which are critical of local authorities, while councillors read only those sections critical of Whitehall. The Audit Commission itself has evolved a 'Fabian' approach: a belief that good management can make a contribution to solving severe social and economic problems, that there is nothing incompatible between *radical* reform and *efficient* reform.

A careful reading of the Audit Commission's reports allows one to jettison a number of ill-founded prejudices. It is not true that all local authorities are inefficient, rather there is a tremendous diversity in the quality of local government, just as schools or firms vary a great deal in their effectiveness.[19] There is no correlation between inefficiency and the political parentage of an authority: there are good and bad Labour, good and bad Conservative, and good and bad Alliance authorities. The most efficient local authorities compare well with successful private companies and compare very favourably with Whitehall and the National Health Service. Despite difficulties in attracting staff, smaller local authorities can be just as efficient as larger authorities. There is much to be achieved by diffusing the best practices of the good authorities, so that the poorer authorities are brought up to scratch. The theme which tends to run through Audit Commission reports is that if local authorities are sometimes run inefficiently, the answer is to reform the local authorities and not to supplant them with central Whitehall control.

As the quote above suggests, local government finance is in a mess. To describe the present system in detail would require a book the size of the Oxford English Dictionary, and it is a well-worn joke that there are only two civil servants in the whole of Whitehall who really know how the system works in its entirety. Nevertheless, we can make some remarks about the consequences of this unncessary complexity. The Public Accounts Committee has described the system for distributing some £10 billion of rate support grant to local authorities to finance the provision of public services as wasteful and inefficient.[20] The capricious nature of the grants means that there is no effective link between local expenditure and local rates, which means that some local authorities are forced into huge rate rises, *despite* reducing their expenditure, while others can raise expenditure without the need for a rise in rates.[21] The system is thus unfair to some local authorities, weakens local accountability and is simultaneously failing in its aim of curbing excessive council spending.

Uncertainty over the effects of the grants system is estimated to cost some £400 million a year in higher rates, as local authorities are required to build up reserves to cope with the vagaries of the system.[22] The rules preventing local authorities from using capital receipts worth over £6 billion from the sale of council houses and other assets have been described by the former head of the Audit Commission as 'Eastern European Planning Laws'.[23] It is estimated that short planning horizons and abrupt changes in the rules on capital expenditure waste more money every year '... than is being spent on the urban programme (£340 million) or on capital spending in the NHS'.[24] The most deprived local authorities in England and Wales suffered a 20 per cent real net reduction in rate support grant between 1982 and 1986, completely dwarfing the assistance received through the urban programme or regional policy. In June 1984, the Audit Commission warned that the complexity of the existing system would lead to an explosion of creative accounting, as we have witnessed in London, Manchester and Liverpool.[25] It pointed to the waste and inefficiency in the system of capital controls in April 1985.[26] Both reports were effectively shelved.

The reason that we have laboured the point that local government finance is in a complete mess is because government ministers have on occasion accused the local authorities of not doing enough to tackle the economic decline in their communities. Local economic initiatives are financed through section 137 of the 1972 Local Government Act which limits a local authority to levying only 2p on the rates for services for which there is no statutory provision. In Cleveland this amounts to £1.5 million, or £25−£30 per unemployed person in the county. If the council spent more than this amount it would be penalised or even taken to court. It is difficult to take seriously the charge by ministers that local authorities do not do enough when they are constrained by the law from doing any more.

In fact, given these financial constraints, it comes as a surprise to learn just how many local authorities have evolved economic development programmes. Councils have for a long time been involved in activities such as the provision of sites and premises, but since the early 1980s they have extended their role with a very diverse array of initiatives (Table 9.3). Most local authorities, whatever their political colours, now have programmes, although few can claim very imaginative or well-developed ones. Sheffield and Cleveland are two of the exceptions, and Table 9.4 outlines some of the initiatives undertaken in Cleveland since the recession. The two characteristics which distinguish local authority initiatives from traditional regional policy are: (1) they were planned locally rather than being imposed by Whitehall; and (2) following on from this, they have placed emphasis on stimulating indigenous economic development

Table 9.3   A Taxonomy of Local Authority Economic Initiatives

Role	Comments
Infrastructure provision	Providing sites and premises, local transport improvement, etc.
Direct aid to businesses	Project assessment and provision of finance; advisory services, e.g. Cleveland's FAS and SBG.
New technology and product development	A new departure involving in Cleveland use of Teesside Polytechnic and Enterprise Agencies to develop new product ideas and assist in applications of new technology.
Promotion and marketing	Helping indigenous businesses in marketing and perhaps attracting inward investment.
Public purchasing 'Contract compliance'	Directing council contracts to local enterprises which comply with certain rules, including the employment of local people.
'Community development'	Equal opportunities, welfare rights and the promotion of 'alternative enterprises' such as co-operatives.
Research and intelligence	Identification of an area's strengths and weaknesses, evaluation of programmes.
Training	Either through specific council initiatives, e.g. VPTS in Cleveland or through MSC schemes.
Recruitment subsidies	For example Cleveland's RPS.

rather than attracting branch plants. It could not be argued that existing initiatives have had a great quantitative impact, if only because the resources going into these programmes have been so small. As the quotation at the beginning of the chapter suggested, all grass-roots initiatives appear to be like trying to drain an ocean with a teaspoon. Nevertheless, the councils have been engaged in a learning exercise and there are a number of lessons to be drawn.

Aside from a lack of resources the organisation of the local authorities has also proved to be a significant barrier. The two-tier system of local government can lead to overlap, duplication and confusion. This is especially true in the provision of advisory services to businesses, where the County Council and the four borough councils in Cleveland appear to be in competition with each other and the 'social entrepreneurs' (Table

Table 9.4 Principal Economic Initiatives Undertaken by Cleveland County Council, 1981–86

Scheme	Comments
Flexible Assistance Scheme (FAS)	As the name suggests, a flexible package of assistance with the council component usually only part of a wider programme of support.
Recruitment Premium Scheme (RPS)	Youth Recruitment Subsidy, available to private employers taking on 18–21 year-olds.
Small Business Grant Scheme (SBG)	Grants of up to £2,000 to enable small firms to buy equipment to expand or consolidate the business (and thereby create or safeguard jobs).
Vocational Preparation and Training Scheme (VPTS)	Up to two years of planned work experience and further education provided by private employers for post-YTS 18- and 19-year-olds.
Council grants to other organisations	Includes support for the Cleveland and Hartlepool Enterprise Agencies, the Co-operative Agency, Information Technology Centre and the CADCAM Centre.
Support for YTS and CP	Over 1,000 16–18-year-olds in County Council YTS schemes (20% of the total). 1,000 employed by County Council on CP (and over 2,500 more by the four Borough Councils).

9.2). Sheffield manages to avoid this because it is a single authority which covers the whole of the city. It has been argued that '. . . the classic problems of local authority organisation — duplication, lack of coordination, slowness of the decision process — emerge with particular force in the economic sphere . . . local authorities' own internal structure, processes and procedures serve to impede rather than to aid the realisation of their economic development aspirations.'[27] The Audit Commission also talks of the problem of the 'committee-ridden bureaucracy',[28] but it can be stressed that authorities such as Sheffield avoid the worst of these problems precisely through reforms to internal organisation.

Most councils are still in the process of building up a skills base and few have the kind of well-staffed economic development department such as exists in Sheffield. Nearly half the Economic Development Officers appointed by local authorities have no supporting professional staff[29] and most admit their lack of professional skills specifically related to this area. The Audit Commission criticises some councillors for indulging in too much political interference in matters best left to council officers.[30] The results can be excessive administrative costs, poor labour relations and a worryingly high turnover in staff. Before this point is pressed too far, however, it should be noted that the relationship between government ministers and the civil service, the teaching profession and the health service workers has not exactly been trouble-free over the recent past. It would seem to be the case that some councillors *and* some Conservative ministers require lessons in how to achieve change through patient negotiation rather than conflict. It is also not wise to press the point that local authorities are sometimes hostile to private enterprise. This is true only for a very small minority of councils, of which Liverpool has become the most notorious. Other Labour authorities such as Glasgow have led the way in evolving the principle of partnership between the public and private sectors.

One of the most innovative departures in the programmes of local authorities has been the evolution of the policy of 'contract compliance' (Table 9.3). Private firms which bid for council contracts have been required to comply with certain rules, the most important of which is that they steer their recruitment towards local residents who are disadvantaged in the normal labour market because of their length of unemployment, a disability, sex or ethnic origin. This policy actually draws on experience in the United States, where contract compliance has been used successfully as an instrument for tackling labour market discrimination against blacks. What research we have to draw upon suggests that private companies do *not* find the requirements imposed by contract compliance rules difficult to fulfill and are not in general resentful of the detailed involvement of local authorities, who are usually no more demanding than private financial institutions.[31] Only attempts by the Greater London Enterprise Board to get firms to increase worker participation in management have been resisted and this may say more about the conservative traditions of British industrial relations than unwelcome state interference.

There has been a growing realisation amongst local authorities that their most powerful instrument for promoting economic development is the *composition* of their entire budget. The idea gaining ground is that all of the operations of a local authority should be reviewed to see how the overall pattern of government expenditure helps to counter, or merely reinforces, the existing imbalances in the labour market. In Chapter 6 we observed that Whitehall's City Action Task Forces had also evolved the principle that the key criterion for backing any initiative was that it should help local disadvantaged people obtain employment. What the task forces and local authorities are agreeing upon is that our premier criterion for judging employment programmes — that they be steered towards those people who are most disadvantaged in the labour market — should be applied to all the services and expenditures of the local authorities, and indeed the public sector as a whole. The financial constraints on local authorities no longer seem so tight if the entire local authority budget is reviewed in order to see if a greater portion of expenditure can be steered towards the long-term unemployed, the disabled, or ethnic minorities.

The concept of contract compliance can be extended not only to firms who are bidding for public contracts, but also to those firms which are in receipt of any kind of public subsidy. Earlier in the chapter we expressed the hope that the local enterprise agencies would be able to build up the skills which would allow them to steer a comprehensive package of assistance to those small businesses which appear most likely to grow into significant employers. The business would have to demonstrate both a good track record and good prospects and would have to show that it had a capacity to sell its service or product outside the immediate locality and preferably outside Britain.[32] In addition, the development contract into which it entered with an agency could require the business to steer its recruitment towards those groups which are being by-passed by the unbalanced recovery. If the firm began to place contracts with components suppliers, there would be an attempt to steer the firm to other local small businesses, so that the purchasing power would not leak out of the community.

It should be stressed that these ideas are already being tried. For many years companies such as Marks and Spencer have been focusing their purchasing power on local suppliers with an insistence on rigorous quality control and the pursuit of good employment practices. In Sweden it is common for large firms to enter into development contracts with local small firms which promise good quality components in return for a steady pattern of purchasing. The 'social entrepreneurs' here in Britain are already engaged in trying to persuade more large firms to enter into this kind of mutually beneficial arrangement. We have already stressed that the most innovative local authorities are seeking to aim their contracts more carefully so as to develop new community enterprises which will be employing disadvantaged local people.

What is needed is an administrative structure and the political commitment to build upon the existing signs of an evolving partnership between private firms, the local authorities and the 'social entrepreneurs' who can act as a bridge.[33] If we look carefully at the range of economic initiatives being carried out by local authorities (Table 9.3) it can be seen that some could easily be contracted out to an enterprise agency, so avoiding the overlap and duplication of bodies which we talked about earlier. These agencies would take over the roles of providing direct aid to business, helping them with product development, marketing and the application of new technology. They could draw on more specialist bodies, such as the higher education institutions or national and regional agencies, for advice in areas where their own expertise was limited (e.g. exporting). They could draw on the local authority, the European Community or private financial institutions to steer capital to firms which have agreed to development contracts.

The local authority would be wise to develop these kinds of bodies rather than seek to administer a development programme all by itself. The authority would still be responsible for evolving an overall strategy based on sound research into local economic strengths and weaknesses and for developing a policy of contract compliance. It should also be stressed that there is very little a regional agency could do that a local authority and its partnership with an enterprise agency could not. A regional body could help provide specialist services, but its role should be essentially supportive. This approach also implies that Whitehall gives local authorities more freedom to pursue the initiatives most suitable to the communities which they represent, rather than presuming that Whitehall knows best and can tell each and every community what it can and cannot do.

These issues are going to be taken up again throughout the third section of this book, but first we want to expand a little more the theme that the private sector has an important role to play in tackling the unbalanced recovery.

Notes

1. A. Cochrane in Anderson *et al.* (1983).
2. See 'The State of the Region Report 1985', from the North of England County Councils Association.

3. The *Department of Employment Gazette*, June 1986, makes the point that there is no correlation beween industrial structure and rates of self-employment.
4. The table was first presented in Storey (1982), p. 196.
5. BSC (Industry) reports that fewer than one in ten of the entrepreneurs it helps are actually ex-steelworkers. Fothergill and Gudgin (1982) also contains an interesting discussion on the factors influencing regional differences in new firm formation. Storey and Johnson (1987) do make the point that up to half of new businesses are started by unemployed people, but mainly in services where displacement is likely to be very high.
6. This result comes out of recent Labour Force Survey estimates of self-employment by region, but these results ought to be treated with some caution.
7. This is emphasised in the chapter by Johnson and Storey in Rajan (1987).
8. The most comprehensive guide to the research on small firms is provided in Storey *et al.* (1987).
9. Storey and Johnson (1987), p. 20.
10. Storey and Johnson (1987), p. 27.
11. The results of survey work on the EAS are contained in the article 'Two years after the enterprise allowance' in the October 1986 edition of the *Department of Employment Gazette*.
12. Public Expenditure White Paper, January 1987. The net cost of the EAS will decline in subsequent years as successful new businesses begin to pay more tax and take on more workers.
13. Storey and Johnson (1987), p. 34.
14. See note 11.
15. The phrase 'social entrepreneurs' was coined by Stephen O'Brien, chief executive of 'Business in the Community', which is the umbrella organisation for the local enterprise agencies.
16. The OECD is the source for these data; see also Storey and Johnson (1987), p. 16.
17. Storey *et al.* (1987) develops just such a set of predictive indicators.
18. From *Faith in the City* (1985), p. 177.
19. See Audit Commission (1986a) *Good Management in Local Government*.
20. See Public Accounts Committee of the House of Commons (1986) *Operation of the Rate Support Grant System*, HMSO.
21. See note 20 and Audit Commission (1984) *Impact on Local Authorities of the Block Grant Distribution System*.
22. Audit Commission (1984).
23. John Banham, now director of the CBI.
24. See Banham (1986).
25. Audit Commission (1984). To argue that a complex system of local government finance will encourage creative accounting by local authorities is exactly equivalent to blaming a complex tax system for encouraging tax avoidance and evasion.
26. Audit Commission (1985) *Capital Expenditure Controls On Local Government in England*.

27. Young and Mill in Hausner (1986), p. 141.
28. Audit Commission (1987) *The Management of London's Authorities: Preventing the Breakdown of Services*, Occasional Paper No 2, HMSO.
29. See Note 27.
30. See Note 28.
31. See Mawson and Miller in Hausner (1986).
32. This is outlined in Storey and Johnson (1987).
33. An example is to be found in the Halifax Community Partnership launched in early 1987.

The Solution

10
The Role of The Private Sector

'. . . it seems unlikely that a job subsidy would make a significant difference to recruitment intentions (which) are primarily geared to demand.'[1]

This chapter must begin with a warning: it is going to contain some fairly complicated economics and a lot of horrible economic jargon. Nevertheless, the argument which is outlined is a fairly clear one and has very important implications for any strategy which is designed to make a significant impact on unemployment. In Chapter 3 we presented our evidence that private employers are very reluctant to hire people who have been out of work for a long time and are instead steering their recruitment predominantly towards labour-market entrants — married women and school leavers. In this chapter we are going to discuss some further evidence which may help to illuminate the attitudes of employers towards pay and jobs. We are going to do this in the context of a proposal which has been around for some time now — the idea of paying a subsidy to employers who recruit someone who has been out of work for more than a year.[2] The proponents of this idea hope that such a subsidy might provide a very powerful incentive to employers to take on the long-term unemployed and re-integrate them into the labour market.

There are two sets of evidence which we can use to look at the idea. The obvious thing to do is to ask employers how they might respond to such a jobs subsidy and we are going to review a number of surveys which have asked questions along these lines. However, it is also true that a number of subsidies have been tried in the past and we are going to look at what impact these subsidies have had. We will use the evidence to see whether we can confidently answer the question: will a subsidy of perhaps £40 or more per man per week, lasting one year,

119

really have a significant impact on persuading employers to recruit the long-term unemployed?

When people put forward the idea of paying such a subsidy they are implicitly suggesting that excessive labour costs are an important factor in preventing firms from taking on more labour. This is at the heart of existing government strategy — that workers are pricing themselves out of jobs by asking for too high wages. In fact, most of the economics profession could be said to be sympathetic, at least in part, to the notion that excessive labour costs are a key factor in explaining high unemployment. It comes as a complete surprise to learn, then, that most employers do *not* blame high wages for their reluctance to recruit! This conclusion flows from the results of a number of surveys of which a Marplan study carried out in 1985 is representative.[3] This company-based survey revealed that 73 per cent of firms were entirely unworried about their recent wage settlements. Only 9 per cent thought that the settlements had worked out too high and 5 per cent thought that they were too low. Similarly, a comprehensive survey of over 3000 companies revealed an equal unwillingness amongst employers to blame excessive labour costs for their reluctance to hire more labour.[4] It is not at all clear how this survey evidence fits the preoccupation of economists with wages, though it would have to be admitted that the profession is generally dismissive of this kind of evidence anyway.[5]

A Gallup survey of 1,041 employers in the Group of Five top industrial nations (the United States, Japan, West Germany, France and Britain) asked companies: what measures would be most effective in generating jobs?[6] A marginal jobs subsidy was suggested as an option, but only one-third of the British employers said that they would participate in such a scheme. Employers in the other countries were slightly more enthusiastic, though it should be noted that employers were not told that such a subsidy could be claimed only if a long-term unemployed person was recruited. A CBI survey[7] of the 1,000 largest British employers and a random sample of 1,000 other firms, conducted in September 1984, revealed that nearly half the companies thought that any reduction in labour costs (by means of a subsidy for example) would make no difference to their recruitment intentions. More than one-third of the employers expressed a vague possibility that reduced labour costs might lead to some additional hiring, but only 9 per cent were certain that it would, and 5 per cent thought lower labour costs would definitely reduce employment! Further research by the CBI, which asks firms quite explicitly if they would respond to a substantial subsidy aimed at the long-term unemployed, reports that for the vast majority of firms such a subsidy would have absolutely no effect on their recruitment intentions. One can see why the CBI spokesman quoted at the beginning of the chapter was so pessimistic about the likely impact of a subsidy.

Now there are criticisms to be made of these surveys. The CBI research was biased towards big manufacturing firms (like ICI) which are indeed unlikely to alter their recruitment in response to a subsidy. Perhaps smaller firms in the service sector would respond more to a reduction in labour costs. However, the evidence presented in Chapter 9 implied that small firms generally steer their recruitment to labour market entrants and this suggests that a subsidy aimed at the long-term unemployed might not have much impact in this sector either. All of this survey evidence is rather dispiriting and on the basis of it alone we can only say that the case for a jobs subsidy is unproven.

This result is going to worry a lot of economists who believe that labour market inflexibility is a prime cause of unemployment. To delve further into this issue would require a whole new book and our immediate concern is with the long-term unemployed and how they might be allowed to compete more effectively in the labour market. It would appear to be the case that the growth of 3 per cent or more a year in real wages in manufacturing since 1983 has been largely compensated for by increased productivity.[8] Firms are flushed with profits and are prepared to pay high wages to retain and motivate an increasingly more skilled core workforce. The cost of additional labour does not appear to be a dominant influence on recruitment: firms are prepared to pay a premium to recruit good workers, but will not take on an unskilled, long-term unemployed individual, no matter how little pay that individual would be prepared to accept. So the long-term unemployed probably *cannot* price themselves into work and neither can the state by offering a subsidy.

To explore this issue further we are going to look at a range of subsidies which have been tried in the past, though most of them were not specifically aimed at the long-term unemployed. Firstly, we are going to have to absorb some economics 'gobbledygook'. A reduction in the cost of labour via a subsidy could increase employment in one of two ways. If labour is cheaper relative to capital (machines), firms might produce a given level of output with more people and fewer machines — this is the 'substitution' effect. In fact we can largely ignore the substitution effect for a temporary employment subsidy, because the mix

of capital and labour is determined over the long term and would not
be influenced by a short-term subsidy. Indeed, there is evidence to
suggest that substitution may not be influenced greatly by labour costs
at all, but is determined by the pace of technological change and the
force of competition.[9]
However, a subsidy may work via an 'output' effect. The reduction
in labour costs will lower total costs. What happens next depends on
the 'incidence' of the subsidy. An employer might use the gain from
these lower costs to reward his workforce with higher wages, or the
gain might be taken in the form of an increase in profits. If the higher
wages and profits are used to increase consumption, then the effect on
employment is going to be rather like offering a tax cut, and in Chapter
1 we discovered that this is a very cost-ineffective way of increasing
employment. The increase in profits might be used to increase investment, but it should be noted that a boom in profits in the mid-1980s in
Britain has not led to a resurgence in investment. Alternatively, the gain
from lower costs may be passed on to the consumer in the form of
lower prices, which may lead to an increased demand for the product.[10]
In improving a firm's price competitiveness the subsidy can act as a 'sur-
rogate depreciation' by making British firms more competitive overseas.
This is the main route by which a subsidy might increase employment,
but it depends crucially on how the firm chooses to use the subsidy and
how it responds to an improvement in competitiveness.[11]
   In judging the effectiveness of a subsidy we also have to consider
'deadweight', 'displacement' and 'wastage'. If a firm uses a subsidy to
employ someone whom it would have recruited anyway, then the subsidy is deadweight — it has not increased employment. If a firm uses
a subsidy to employ one person, but fires another who is not covered
by the subsidy, this is called displacement. If a firm uses a subsidy to
lower its prices, but merely puts other British firms under competitive
pressure so that they have to reduce employment, this is another form
of displacement.[12] If a firm hires someone using a subsidy but then
fires him once the subsidy has come to an end, this is called 'wastage'.
After we have taken into account all of these factors we arrive at an estimate of the *net incremental effect*. If we subsidise one hundred jobs,
but fifty would have been created anyway (deadweight) and thirty are
displacing other workers, then the net incremental effect is 20 per cent.
   Table 10.1 gives the estimated net cost of creating jobs under various
employment subsidies, given three different assumptions about the net
incremental effect. To illustrate we shall consider the effectiveness of

Table 10.1 The Effects of Special Employment Subsidies

	Net Incremental Effect		
Net cost per job created under:	*10%*	*20%*	*40%*
Small Firms Employment Subsidy	6,580	3,290	1,645
Young Workers Scheme	4,800	2,400	1,200
Recruitment Premium Scheme	5,200	2,600	1,300
£40-per-week Employment Subsidy	13,870	6,940	3,470

the Small Firms Employment Subsidy which paid £20 per week for six months for each additional employee taken on, when it operated in the late 1970s. Initially only small manufacturing firms in the assisted areas were eligible, but the scope of the subsidy was gradually extended to the whole country, the services sector and firms employing up to two hundred workers. The most detailed evaluation of the subsidy suggested that the net incremental effect was 40 per cent and half of the new jobs survived the subsidy.[13] If this is true then the subsidy was very cost-effective indeed, though this did not stop the incoming government in 1979 from scrapping it.

The new administration was soon to replace a number of existing subsidies with the Young Workers Scheme, which paid employers a subsidy for hiring people under the age of eighteen, provided wages were less than £40 per week. The aim of the subsidy was not only to lower labour costs but also to lower the expectations of young workers by emphasising low pay for teenagers. This made the scheme very controversial, especially as evidence was presented that there was a significant amount of displacement taking place, with firms using the subsidy to hire teenagers and fire adult workers. The net incremental effect of the subsidy may have been as low as 10 per cent.[14] With the institution of the Youth Training Scheme, the Young Workers Scheme was clearly in direct competition for sixteen- and seventeen-year-olds. It has been superseded by the New Workers Scheme aimed at the 18-20 age group which also emphasises low pay (less than £55 per week for teenagers, less than £65 per week for twenty-year olds). No proper evaluation has been conducted on the effects of this scheme, but it seems likely that displacement is once again going to be important and the net incremental effect may work out rather low.

In the late 1960s and early 1970s a Regional Employment Premium was paid to manufacturing firms in the assisted areas for each person employed. It subsidised the total stock of employment, rather than subsidising the additional or marginal worker. It thus operated in a similar fashion to recent proposals for charging lower employers' national insurance contributions in regions of high unemployment. A survey of 300 firms in receipt of the subsidy suggested that, nationally, only 35-50,000 jobs were created by the premium between 1968 and 1971 and this amounts to only one in eight of the jobs delivered by regional policy as a whole in this period.[15] The subsidy did not lead to any significant substitution of labour for capital and, given that it was spread so thinly across total employment, it hardly altered the marginal cost of increasing production, so that the output effect was also limited. Half of the incidence of the subsidy was passed on in the form of lower prices and the increase in profits allowed by the premium did lead to some additional investment.

One very interesting result is that only one-third of firms in receipt of the subsidy had a clear strategy for using it. Nevertheless, six out of ten firms said the premium had increased employment. This suggests that if you ask firms how they will respond to a subsidy, they may underestimate its effect. A firm answering a survey may not take account of the fact that a subsidy might also be increasing the output of other firms, generating demand which will boost the original firm's output.[16] Only when a firm is in actual receipt of a subsidy will we be able to measure its impact on employment. This may lead us to qualify our earlier statements about the results of the surveys of employers' intentions. However, a review of the arguments and evidence by the OECD concluded that '... the issue of cutting employer payroll taxes so as to stimulate employment is a complicated one, for which it is difficult to make robust predictions of the size and timing of the effects.'[17]

It may come as a surprise to learn that by 1984 there were some thirty local authorities offering recruitment subsidies to private employers, indicating that Whitehall is not the only institution active in this field.[18] Cleveland County was something of a pioneer and in the early 1980s was operating two separate subsidies.[19] The Recruitment Premium Scheme (RPS) was instituted in January 1981; it paid £30 per week for six months to employers taking on young people under twenty who had been out of work for more than a year. The Cleveland Assistance Scheme for Employment (CASE), instituted in February 1982, was aimed at adults unemployed for over twenty-six weeks and paid up to

30 per cent of the gross wage for six months for employees who were additional to the workforce. Both subsidies were discretionary rather than automatic and required assurance from the employer that the jobs were additional (to minimise deadweight) and would outlast the subsidy. What is very interesting for our purposes is that RPS has been a modest success, while CASE did not live up to expectations and was discontinued in July 1983.

Between 1981 and 1984, over four hundred young people had obtained permanent employment under the RPS. This figure takes into account jobs which did not survive the subsidy, but does not include any estimate of possible deadweight or displacement. Despite the efforts to ensure that the employees were additional to the workforce, some deadweight was bound to occur and, given that most of the jobs were in services, the displacement of existing employment may also have been rather high. Nevertheless, we might conclude that the net incremental effect was likely to have been higher than for the Young Workers Scheme and may have approached the 40 per cent achieved by the Small Firms Employment Subsidy, making the RPS a useful and cost-effective subsidy.

In the eighteen months of its existence CASE supported only 171 jobs in total, well below its hoped-for target. The subsidy was widely marketed, including a direct mail shot to 8,000 local firms. However, only one-third of private enquiries became applications for assistance as firms realised that they were not eligible for the subsidy because they intended to create the jobs anyway, because they considered the subsidy inadequate, or could not guarantee the job would survive the subsidy. Forty per cent of all applications were turned down by the authority because it was not satisfied that the firm intended to create wholly new jobs or there were doubts about the firm's financial position.

There are two possible explanations why the RPS significantly out-performed the CASE. Firstly, the RPS was administered by the County Careers Service, while CASE was administered by the County Planning Department. The Careers Service had spent many years building up a relationship with local employers as part of its job of placing young people in employment. It also had a clear idea of the skills and aptitudes of the teenagers on its books. The highly experienced staff were thus able to use the subsidy to place the right young people with the right employer. The planners were entirely new to the field of placing people with employers and their relationship with the companies was less well founded. This suggests that it is very important to get the administrative agency right for distributing any subsidy. In particular the officials involved must have detailed knowledge of local employers. This raises worries about the MSC administering any jobs subsidy because of the habit of frequently moving MSC staff between posts, with the consequence that the kind of long-term relationships with employers which proved advantageous to the Careers Service are just not there.

A second explanation for the relative failure of the CASE is even more worrying. The RPS was aimed at young people, the CASE at the older long-term unemployed. We have discussed at length the preference shown by firms towards recruiting young people anyway and in this sense the RPS was merely reinforcing the existing trend in the labour market. The subsidy provided by the CASE was not enough to overcome the barriers which have been erected by employers against recruiting the long-term unemployed. The experience of other local authorities reinforces this lesson.[20] In general, firms are pleased to use a subsidy to recruit young people or the short-term unemployed, but far less willing to take on people who have been out of work for a long time. Evidence from Manchester suggests that firms have used subsidies to recruit on the edges of the conurbation, but have been far more reluctant to increase employment in the more depressed inner cities. When considered alongside the evidence from surveys on employers' attitudes, the actual experience of various subsidies suggests that payments to employers to take on people are not a very effective instrument for dealing with the unbalanced recovery. Instead, they may simply reinforce the existing patterns of recruitment in the labour market, and a subsidy aimed specifically at the older long-term unemployed adults may not be able to alter employers' attitudes significantly.

Work carried out by the Department of Employment on the idea of offering a £40 per week subsidy for twelve months to any employer taking on a long-term unemployed person suggests that the net incremental effect would only be 20 per cent.[21] More than half the jobs supported would be created anyway (deadweight) and there would also be significant substitution. Perhaps up to a quarter of a million extra long-term unemployed people would be helped into jobs, displacing 120,000 other workers. There would be a net increase in employment of 130,000 at a net cost of about £7,000 per job. The total net cost to the Exchequer would be nearly one billion pounds. Nevertheless it should be noted that, even if the net incremental effect is only 20 per cent, a cost of £7,000 per job still makes a subsidy at least six times more cost-effective than income-tax cuts.

At this point it is worth summarising what we have learnt so far. Employers do not seem to blame excessive labour costs for their reluctance to hire the unemployed and this throws doubt on the preoccupation of economists with wages. However, to argue that high *real* wages are not a major cause of unemployment is not to deny that, if output were to grow at a much faster pace than the 3 per cent per annum seen since 1983, this might lead to upward pressure on *nominal* wage growth and a faster pace of inflation. This suggests the need to pay attention to instruments, such as an incomes policy, which can be held in reserve to counter such a wages problem. This is entirely different from stressing the need to cut wages. Why are firms unworried about their labour costs and therefore unresponsive to wage subsidies? It would seem to be the case that firms are concerned about building up a skilled core workforce and this explains their unwillingness to recruit the long-term unemployed who, we discovered in Chapter 3, may not possess significant skills.

Thus a strategy aimed at persuading private employers to take on the long-term unemployed must also contain a substantial training component to deliver the skills which are most attractive to employers, and in Chapter 12 we are going to develop this theme in the context of a review of the performance of the existing education and training system in Britain. For the moment we would like to return briefly to the argument presented in Chapter 9 about the possible use of contract compliance. Firms in receipt of public contracts or public subsidies should be required to steer their recruitment towards the long-term unemployed and other individuals who are disadvantaged in the labour market. This contractual requirement could be accompanied by the use of subsidies for employment and training, to form a Development Contract emphasising a combined 'stick and carrot' approach.[22] It is very important that such an approach should emphasise the advantages to the community as a whole of a fairer distribution of employment. It is in the employers' interest to see that the long-term unemployed are not bypassed by the unbalanced recovery, and private firms ought to recognise that they must play a role.

We should also take note from the experience of Cleveland's subsidy experiments that it is very important to get the administrative agency for these schemes right. The role of the Careers Service in Cleveland could be widely emulated, and a subsidy operated by Careers Services across the country could replace the New Workers Scheme as the primary instrument for placing post-YTS teenagers in employment. This would fit in well with the proposals in Chapter 12 for ending the unnecessary division of responsibility for education and training between the Departments of Employment and Education by establishing a single Department of Education and Training which would of course cover the Careers Service too. We will develop the argument that (for the moment) the MSC concentrates on adult long-term unemployment, leaving the problems of young people to a single Department to stress the continuity between school and work, education and training. It would be hoped that, given time and a concentration of effort, the MSC might build up the kind of long-term relationships with employers characteristic of the Careers Service, which would enable a more successful placement of the long-term unemployed with private firms.

The private sector has an important role to play in helping to counter the unbalanced recovery, but in the next chapter we are going to explore the responsibility of the public sector to the long-term unemployed.

Notes

1. Peter Lobban of the CBI on p.191 of Hart (1986).
2. The clearest statement of this proposal is contained in the chapter 'A new deal for the long-term unemployed' by Layard, Metcalf and O'Brien in Hart (1986).
3. Reported in *The Financial Times*, 21 October 1985.
4. This is the Institute of Manpower Studies Report published as Rajan and Pearson (1986).
5. If real-world facts conflict with an economist's model, it is the real world which must be wrong. Less cynically, we outline elsewhere in the chapter the reasons for viewing survey evidence cautiously.
6. Reported in *The Financial Times Survey*, 'Work : the way ahead', 24 July 1986.
7. This survey is discussed in Standing (1986), pp.51 and 62.
8. This point is also made by Professor Alan Budd in the *Charter For Jobs Economic Report*, 'Policies towards incomes and employment', Vol.2. No.8, May 1987.
9. See, for example, the parable related by Michael Prowse in *The Financial Times*, 13 March 1986. The textiles giant Courtaulds said that it would not reverse its policy of redundancies, no matter how significant a wage cut its workers accepted. The decision to introduce labour-shedding technology was related to the need to keep up with competitors and open up new product lines for major customers. Labour costs were irrelevant.
10. Especially if product demand is price-elastic.
11. An improvement in price competitiveness will not work if the problem lies in non-price competitiveness, i.e. poor marketing, bad design, low quality, and so on.

12. We have not bothered to mention the 'domino' effect where a firm claims a subsidy because another firm has done so.
13. Layard (1979).
14. See the submission by the Institute of Manpower Studies to the House of Commons Employment Committee, printed on 29 January 1986, HMSO.
15. This is the survey reported by Moore and Rhodes in 'A quantitative analysis of the effects of the Regional Employment Premium and other regional policy instruments' in Whiting (1976).
16. This is a classic example of an external benefit from a subsidy.
17. See pp.102 — 104 of the OECD Employment Outlook, September 1986.
18. See Botham (1984b). Botham (1984a) also contains a useful discussion of marginal employment subsidies.
19. This section draws on the paper by Gunby (1984) and on the author's conversation with Ray Hurst, head of the Cleveland Careers Service.
20. See Botham (1984b).
21. These results are reported in a Memorandum by the Director-General to the NEDC, 20 February 1987, 'The British Labour Market and Unemployment'.
22. Under this arrangement, the employer has a triple incentive to hire : a contractual obligation, a subsidy for recruitment and another for training. The fly in the ointment here is that strict contract compliance or 'local labour' clauses may not be legal under European Community rules.

11

The Economics of Balanced Recovery

'What gets me, all this work needs to be done and all these builders and electricians out of work. Why won't they let them do the work? I mean they pay dole money out, why don't they pay them money to have them do something?'[1]

It is a cruel paradox that many of the long-term unemployed live in communities which are also scarred by bad housing, inadequate social services and poor schools. We have at one and the same time massive unmet social need and several million people without work. The question which keeps running through the minds of many people is, why can't we match the unemployed to the tasks which need to be done in the very communities in which the unemployed live?

To answer this question we are going to look at three key areas of public-sector activity: housing, energy conservation, and community health and social services. We have focused on these areas for three reasons. Firstly, as we shall show, investment in them would seem to satisfy all of the criteria which we set out in Chapter 1 for evaluating the impact on employment of any policy. Secondly, they illustrate the chaotic mess which now characterises the finance and organisation of the public sector in Britain, the outcome of the civil war between local and central government first referred to in Chapter 9, damagingly irrelevant financial controls and organisational structures which make less sense as each year passes. Thirdly, they also illustrate the consequences of having a government nominally hostile to the public sector, but which allows a tremendous waste of public resources by failing to recognise that it is the *composition* of public-sector activity which matters for economic efficiency and social justice and not a summary statistic such as government expenditure as a proportion of gross domestic product.

In looking at these three key areas we are going to draw on the results of independent research by such bodies as the Policy Studies Institute and the Audit Commission. We have thus avoided, as far as possible, relying on the work of lobby groups which might be said to have a vested interest. In this way we hope to rise above the political civil war and offer, as far as our knowledge allows, an objective assessment of the state of affairs in these three services. Our analysis will try to follow a logical structure in first outlining the scale of the problem of unmet need, then looking at the existing policy response and finally outlining the kind of changes which may be necessary if we are to provide effective public services which also play a role in countering the unbalanced recovery. However, it does seem necessary to add one further caveat. I am not suggesting that as an economist I am qualified to plan the future of these services. Rather, I want to suggest that it is important to focus on whether the public sector as a whole is acting to reinforce or counter the imbalances in the labour market which have been described in this book.

Let us look first at the state of housing in Britain, which is a considerable political football. The Audit Commission has estimated that the backlog of repairs in the local authority housing stock is over £20 billion (equivalent to 5 per cent of GDP).[2] However, contrary to popular belief, the private housing stock is in an even worse state of repair. A house in London is defined as unsatisfactory if it is unfit for human habitation, lacking in one or more basic amenities, or requires over £5,300 in repair work. On the basis of this definition about 15 per cent of the capital's public housing stock is unsatisfactory, but so is 21 per cent of owner-occupied housing, and fully 47 per cent of private rented accommodation.[3] Over half a million houses lie within this definition in London with the greatest concentration, in terms of absolute numbers, in the owner-occupied sector. Bad housing is most likely to be owned or rented by an elderly person or someone who is unemployed or on a very low income.

If we focus on public housing, the Audit Commission is very critical of the management of council estates by many local authorities. Repair and maintenance services are often inefficiently organised, with far too much reactive maintenance and not enough repair work planned carefully in advance. Some authorities charge rents at levels which are too low to cover the costs of maintenance and are slow in dealing with the problem of rent arrears. There are delays in re-letting vacant properties and some authorities appear to have abnormally high administrative overheads. These problems, which can be laid at the door of the local authorities, are compounded by the waste and complexity inherent in the system of capital controls imposed by Whitehall which, we learned in Chapter 9, waste more money than is spent on the entire urban programme or on capital spending in the NHS. The Audit Commission has, to no avail, stressed the need for regular assessment of housing needs and stable investment programmes with at least a three-year planning period. There is also a growing need to provide appropriate housing for the elderly and disabled and to attend to the increased numbers of one-parent families and the problem of growing homelessness.

The state already devotes some £14 billion to the housing budget in Britain, equivalent to $3\frac{1}{2}$ per cent of gross domestic product.[4] Of this total, some £4.75 billion is spent on mortgage interest tax relief, some £2.5 billion is lost through exempting house sales from capital gains tax, £1 billion is spent in subsidising the sale of council housing, over £3 billion goes in housing benefit, and only £2.6 billion is actually spent on investment in the housing stock. This is a massive misallocation of public resources and the most elementary economics would suggest that the artificial pumping up of housing demand through the use of indiscriminate subsidies, combined with restrictions on housing supply, is bound to lead to house price inflation. In addition we have the 'Eastern European Planning Laws' which forbid local authorities the use of the receipts from sales of assets for investment in the housing stock. Local authorities are also hampered in funding the training programmes aimed at building skills, despite the evidence that the public sector is almost alone in training apprentices in the construction trades. [5] The skills base necessary to underpin the construction industry is being lost.

Housing policy needs to be considered as a whole, and the most imaginative and comprehensive programme for reform was outlined in 1985.[6] It would involve the phased abolition of mortgage interest tax relief and the rationalisation of all the other subsidies into one tenure-neutral, income-related housing allowance, which would help cover rent and mortgage payments and maintenance costs for households on average or below average incomes. The losers under this redistribution would be households earning more than £12-15,000 a year, who arguably ought to be able to manage without public subsidy anyway. Councils would be free to spend their accumulated capital receipts on investment in improving the local authority housing stock, with a scheme to redistribute receipts to those authorities in most need. In addition a reformed system of improvement grants would be aimed at the poor and elderly in the private sector. Council housing letting procedures and maintenance services would be decentralised to the level of individual estates and made responsive to tenants' organisations. The local authorities would be responsible for the overall co-ordination of housing provision in their areas, but would increasingly rely on 'third-sector' bodies such as the housing associations to build and maintain housing.

A considerable re-allocation of resources towards housing investment and away from subsidies satisfies all our criteria. Housing repair is particularly labour-intensive and therefore cost-effective in reducing unemployment; by improving the physical environment, especially for poorer households, it delivers obvious social benefits; it is work which can be organised quite quickly; it has low import content and it is precisely the kind of employment which can be aimed at the long-term unemployed. Investment in many hundreds of small-scale programmes makes far more sense than vast infrastructure projects of the channel tunnel or Humber bridge variety. There is also something rather attractive about helping the long-term unemployed to improve the physical environment in their own communities, addressing the priorities set by the unemployed themselves for increased resources. Of course, the existing Community Programme performs some rehabilitative work and in doing so employs people who have been without a job for a long time but, as we explained in Chapter 7, the 'two-year rule' makes this kind of work necessarily of marginal value. The only way to have a rational and planned programme of housing renovation is to allow reformed local authorities the financial latitude to construct a strategy relevant to the communities which they represent, while steering any employment, including the jobs provided by 'third-sector' bodies or private contractors, to those who are most disadvantaged in the labour market.

Every winter this country agonises over media reports about the suffering of the elderly from the cold. By spring the moral outrage tends to fizzle out so that in the next winter the agony is repeated. The organisations which work with the elderly are angry that preventative measures are not undertaken and it has to be said that energy conservation remains a neglected, underfunded, cinderella service.

There has been no major survey to discover how many elderly people are at risk from a cold winter for some fifteen years. It would be too cynical to suggest that no-one in authority appears to want to find out. A 1972 survey suggested that 850,000 elderly people in Britain were at risk and there are no reasons to believe that the problem has grown smaller.[7] The poor and the elderly not only live in the worst repaired housing, their homes usually have the most inefficient forms of heating and often lack simple conservation measures such as draught-proofing. However, these people tend not to have access to capital to make the necessary investment in appropriate heating and conservation, which would over the years yield significant savings in energy costs and produce a marked improvement in the quality of the home environment.[8] What information we have suggests that fully one half of all homes has inadequate roof insulation, 90 per cent lack cavity wall insulation and 85 per cent lack simple draught-proofing.[9] One in five houses, many of them owned by the elderly, relies on peak rate electric heating which is twice as expensive as gas-fired heating. Very simple conservation measures such as draught-proofing, cavity wall and hot water cylinder insulation, have an initial capital cost of about £500 as a package for an average home and this is paid back through savings in energy costs in under four years. The installation of simple heating controls and the replacement of electric with gas fires also have low capital costs and a short pay-back period.

Government policy in this area is hampered by a lack of coordination between agencies. The Departments of Energy, Environment, Health and Social Security and the MSC indulge in the same squabbling, overlap and duplication for which the local authorities are often blamed. Like most British institutions, these agencies take an incredibly short-term view and focus only upon the gross costs of capital investment, neglecting to take into account the net savings from reduced energy.costs and social security payments. The DHSS spent £400 million in 1986 on heating allowances for households on supplementary benefit (akin to the housing subsidies described earlier).[10] The social security system also paid the pathetic sum of £1.7 million in severe weather payments which can be claimed during the winter months providing a very complex set of criteria is satisfied. Less than 10 per cent of those elderly people eligible for these payments claim them, either because they are unaware of their existence, find the rules too confusing, or are simply unable or unwilling to tramp down to the local DHSS office in the middle of winter. From 1988 the heating allowances are to be fused into the new Income Support Scheme and the severe weather payments are to be absorbed into the new Social Fund. As this is cash-limited, there is the interesting possibility of DHSS offices simply running out of money in the middle of a particularly severe winter and having to refuse all applications, no matter how desperate the circumstances of the individual.

In 1979 local authorities carried out simple insulation and draught-proofing on 590,000 homes. In 1986 they managed 82,000, or one-seventh as many. The local authority programmes have fallen victim to the same confusing capital controls which were described in Chapter 9 and which have proved so damaging in the field of housing. The Home Insulation Scheme which offers grants of up to 90 per cent for roofing insulation had its budget cut from £33 million to £23 million in 1986 (Energy Efficiency Year). The maximum grant under the scheme has been fixed at £95 since 1978 and has thus been halved in real terms. As one would expect, the MSC is in on the act. Neighbourhood Energy Action is the umbrella charity for 360 local projects which find people on supplementary benefit who need assistance, help them to claim government grants and then, using labour paid for under the Community Programme, perform simple conservation work. By the end of 1987 up to 8,000 long-term unemployed people might be at work on these CP schemes. However, this is only scratching the surface of the problem and from 1988 this kind of activity,too, will be dependent on payments from the Social Fund.

We have a picture of organisational chaos in existing policy which betrays any sense of strategy or view of this kind of work as a social priority. Yet the kind of simple but comprehensive energy measures we have been describing appear to satisfy all our criteria. They are certainly cost-effective, especially when viewed over a period of more than one year and in terms of net costs. Organising this work requires little advanced planning or long construction lead times and is particularly labour-intensive (unlike building nuclear power stations). The work has a very low import intensity and, in the long run, reduces the need to import energy or run down fossil fuels. There should be no need to stress the social benefit in helping those people who suffer most from inadequate heating and there are wider benefits to be gained from reduced pollution and the improvement of the environment. Above all this kind of work is eminently suitable for the long-term unemployed in that it does not require an unnecessarily high level of skills. Once again there is something attractive about employing individuals who have been out of work for a long time in helping the poorest people in the community improve the quality of their lives by raising the standard of the home environment.

A programme of fundamental reform would begin by changing the statutes of the energy utilities, to shift the emphasis away from energy supply to energy conservation.[11] One suggested scheme would involve a utility carrying out an energy audit on a domestic customer, providing finance free of interest to cover the cost of conservation measures and then automatically recovering the outlay from savings in the energy bill. The customer would pay no extra and would ultimately be presented with an energy-saving house. The utilities in the United States are already required to provide this kind of service. Another idea would involve a private consortium of energy consultants, contractors and banking institutions contracting to upgrade public buildings at their own expense. The consortium would take over a building for a period of, say, five years during which it would receive from the public authority a payment equivalent to five years' normal energy bills. The consortium would invest in whatever conservation measures were appropriate and any savings in energy costs over five years would be its own. The public authority would be presented after this period with an energy-efficient building at no public cost. The European Community has noted that this kind of 'third-party financing' arrangement is being stifled by the '... illogical treatment by the UK Treasury of third-party financing as public borrowing when the public sector makes no initial investment and takes no risks'.[12]

Reformed local authorities would play the same kind of co-ordinating and enabling role which they should be encouraged to develop in the field of housing. They would build upon the existing infrastructure offered by the organisations such as Neighbourhood Energy Action and would seek to contract out work to third parties. A community approach could be adopted involving the designation of areas in which the activities of all organisations involved in promoting, financing or carrying out energy conservation or housing rehabilitation were coordinated in one rolling programme. Any private or charitable bodies engaged in this work would be subject to the kind of contract compliance rules outlined in Chapters 9 and 10. In this way the employment generated by a programme of energy conservation would be steered towards the long-term unemployed even if the jobs were being created in private-sector bodies. On the most conservative assumptions, between 50,000 and 100,000 jobs could be created[13] and made available largely to people who have been out of work for a long time or are in some other way disadvantaged in the labour market.

In the past two decades there has evolved a strategy for moving the elderly, the mentally ill and the mentally handicapped out of large and impersonal Victorian institutions and into care organised in the community. In principle this is a humane idea, but there is a mounting body of concern that in practice its implementation is proving nothing short of disastrous. The Audit Commission emphasises that this is the consequence both of a shortage of resources devoted to community care and a tragically confused administrative structure which is responsible for implementing the shift to this form of care.[14]

The existing long-stay institutions are the responsibility of the District Health Authorities, but the provision of supportive services is the task of the social services departments which are answerable to the county councils. The organisation of sheltered housing falls to the borough councils. In addition, there are a plethora of voluntary organisations active in the field, many of them receiving funding through the Community Programme which, as we explained in Chapter 7, implies that the MSC is also making decisions about social priorities. This organisational mess means that, when individuals are discharged from an institution or hospital, many simply fall through the net and onto the streets. No one agency has responsibility for each individual case and the boundaries of district health authorities and local authorities do not coincide, roles get confused and the two-tier system of local government implies that the agency responsible for providing social workers or home helps is not the same agency responsible for organising appropriate housing.

Let us be clear about the consequences of this. Some of the most vulnerable people in our society are being effectively dumped without the benefit of sheltered housing or adequate supporting services, with the result that many desperate individuals try to get readmitted into the very institutions from which they have been discharged. Community Care implies a shift in expenditure from the health to the local authorities, but in practice the machinery for achieving this redistribution does not work. Hard-pressed health authorities are reluctant to part with the money released by closing old long-stay hospitals and the local authorities are so tightly constrained by the complex and wasteful central controls on capital and current spending that they are unable to build up adequate supportive services in the community. Existing Treasury rules prevent health authorities from borrowing against the site value of old long-stay hospitals scheduled for closure, which when sold can be worth millions. Local authorities which devote more resources to community care may end up being penalised by Whitehall for going beyond their spending limits. The Audit Commission Report which heavily criticised many inner-London authorities for poor management nevertheless praised them for their '... determination to make such provision (for community care) despite the high cost of doing so.'[15]

If community care is not to degenerate with tragic consequences we first need to tackle the organisational mess described above. The Audit Commission has suggested making local authorities solely responsible for coordinating provision for the mentally handicapped, the health authorities responsible for the mentally ill, with joint boards to look after the elderly. Arguably we need to go further. The separation of health care and the provision of social services and the division of responsibility for housing and social work between county and borough councils is illogical and inefficient. The answer would lie in single-tier local authorities and the adaptation of health authority boundaries to match those of the new local authorities, with a view to possible merger in the very long run. This takes us into the field of local government reform which we will address in more detail in Chapter 13.

On the basis of all our criteria, enhanced support for community care within a reformed organisational structure scores very highly indeed. The provision of employment in this field can be organised on a reasonable time scale and is very labour-intensive, making it a cost-effective instrument. There is once again no need to stress the social benefit of supporting services aimed at the most vulnerable members of our society. It is work which is eminently suitable for the long-term unemployed and other people who are disadvantaged in the labour market. Once again we have the image of unemployed people doing work in their own communities and in providing help and companionship to vulnerable individuals in the community. An infusion of resources here can be seen to provide help for two large sections of society which are being by-passed by growing economic prosperity: the unemployed and the people who need community care. The more innovative local authorities are already moving towards the decentralisation of social services with the emphasis upon the organisation of facilities at the level of individual communities, responsive to local feelings and employing local people.

In this conception of community care there is no obvious place for the MSC or the provision of purely temporary posts. In the social services field we emphasised in Chapter 7 the importance of establishing long-term career-client relationships and we have stressed the need to allow for the long-term planning of community care provision. A labour

board or training agency is not qualified to determine priorities here and
we are suggesting that the large part of the Community Programme aimed
at social provision, including the support for voluntary agencies, ought
to be integrated with the rest of local authority provision in this area.[16]

We have now looked at three public services and illustrated how much-
needed reforms in the finance and organisation of those services could
deliver both more effective provision and increased employment which
could be steered towards the long-term unemployed. The more general
principle which we are pushing is that in deciding which areas deserve
priority for additional public resources we should pay paramount attention to the needs of all those people who are being bypassed by the
economic recovery. These include the most disadvantaged members of
the community who want to work and those who cannot work because
of age, disability or handicap. We want to overcome the paradox noted
at the beginning of the chapter: massive unmet social need and millions
out of work. We are suggesting that each public body should review
the services it provides and ask whether the massive expenditure
emanating from the public sector is correctly targeted on the poorer
members of the community.[17] In Chapter 9 we noted that some local
authorities are coming around to think of the activities of the public sector in this way and we believe that all public bodies might begin to emulate
this approach.

There is a precedent. Despite thirty years of the existence of the
National Health Service, in the 1970s an increasing body of research
was coming to light which suggested that certain regions of the country
were being provided with less than their fair share of health care resources
on the basis of need in those communities. The result was the Resource
Allocation Working Party (RAWP), instituted in 1976 with the explicit
aim of redistributing health service resources in accordance with each
region's need. The spread of health services was no longer to be based
on the historical accidents which left some regions (particularly London) with an over-generous provision of resources, while other areas
were relatively under-provided. A recent review of the progress of
RAWP concluded that it has been a unique, if qualified, success and
'... represents perhaps the most sophisticated and objective system in
the world for establishing the fair share of health resources ...' to which
individual communities are entitled.[18]

It is not precisely clear why RAWP has been so singularly successful, but one should not underestimate the importance of the consensus which was generated surrounding the broad objectives of RAWP. The initiative was instituted by a Labour government, but was carried on under a Conservative administration without any attempt at back-tracking. RAWP has never become a party political football in the way that housing, education, employment, or just about any other policy area you might care to name, have fallen victim to cheap party politics. Senior NHS management was brought into the construction of RAWP at an early stage so that this was not a case of politicians or top civil servants imposing their will on the people managing a service at the point of contact with the public. The contrast with the approach of successive Education Secretaries to the reform of schools and colleges could not be greater, as we shall see in the next chapter. RAWP appears to be a successful case study in how to achieve change by constructing a consensus.

What might be the impact if all public services were to have their priorities re-ordered in a similar fashion? We are suggesting that the public sector as a whole should consider whether the existing pattern of public expenditure reinforces or counters the unbalanced recovery. This would imply looking at the regional pattern of spending for each department and at whether the recruiting practices of the department might be steered more towards the long-term unemployed. The public sector may have to lead the way in setting good employment practices which can be emulated by the private sector.

There are other ways in which public-sector activity might be reorientated. Increasingly, private firms are moving their decision making to London and the greater South-East. This concentration of economic power is somewhat unique amongst the western industrialised nations and probably reflects the over-centralisation of political and administrative control in London. The concentration of power in Whitehall must also have an impact on the way in which the unbalanced recovery is being ignored, for the plight of communities away from London, or buried in corners of the capital itself, is not readily noticeable in the corridors of power. If the private sector is to be encouraged to spread its business intelligence, marketing, research and development and control functions more widely across the nation, once again the public sector may have to lead the way.

In 1973 the Hardman Report proposed the dispersal of 31,000 London-based civil service jobs to the regions.[19] However, the momentum for this programme was never realised and, having mentioned the Vehicle

Licensing Centre in Swansea or the DHSS Computer Centre at New-castle, one runs out of obvious examples of successful decentralisation. A proposal to move the Property Services Agency to Middlesbrough, where it would have provided 3,000 valuable white-collar jobs, was reversed in 1979. One of the most interesting examples of dispersal was the move of the Manpower Services Commission itself to Sheffield. Over a period of time, the resources saved by selling off a central-London site and no longer having to compensate staff for inner-London living expenses can more than pay for new buildings in the destination area and the transitional costs of moving.

It is hard to see why many of the ministries concerned with domestic policy need to be established in the capital, especially when given the improvements in telecommunications, information technology and transport. The Departments dealing with Health, the Environment, Education, Agriculture, Employment, and so on, might well consider whether their functions could not easily be carried out elsewhere. It is important that over time the recruitment policies of such departments come to reflect the balance of employment opportunities in the com-munities in which they reside. Setting up the MSC in Sheffield is in itself not enough if the jobs which are provided reinforce the position of the suburban enclaves rather than inner-city residents. Even those public bodies which remain in London ought to consider their responsibility to the people who live in Brixton, Tower Hamlets or Islington, rather than give employment opportunities only to commuters.

Other areas of government activity might also embrace the concept of affirmative action in favour of those at present by-passed by the recovery. The privatisation initiatives of the 1980s have not only missed out on the opportunity to stimulate greater competition in certain in-dustries, but have missed a golden opportunity to establish strong regional concerns. It is not too late to break up British Telecom into regional bodies on the pattern of the deregulation of the American telecommunica-tions market, allowing unlimited competition. The TSB flotation could have been used to create regional banks, again on the US model, and so stem the tide towards the centralisation of financial services in Lon-don. At the very least the remaining nationalised industries, and those privatised concerns subject to regulatory control, should be required to fulfill contract compliance rules and steer their employment towards the most disadvantaged in the labour market. British competition policy, especially with regard to mergers, needs overhauling any way and in discussing whether mergers are beneficial or not, questions relating to the distribution of employment gains or losses and the prevention of further centralisation of decision making in London deserve consideration. In Chapter 13 we are going to discuss further some of the political implications of what we have been discussing in this book. For the moment we are left with the principle of economic justice which underlines the arguments presented here: any policy instrument should be judged first and foremost on what it achieves for those individuals with the fewest advantages and what it does to promote a more even distribution of the gains from economic prosperity.

Notes

1. A worker on Teesside, quoted in Foord *et al.* (1985).
2. One can refer to various Audit Commission Reports: *Managing the Crisis in Council Housing* (1986b), *Improving Council House Maintenance* (1986c) and *The Management of London's Authorities: Preventing the Breakdown of Services* (1987), Occasional Paper No. 2. See also Banham (1986).
3. The survey of London's housing stock was reported in *The Economist*, 14 March 1987. Another useful reference is *Housing: Twenty-Five Popular Fallacies* by Kleineman *et al.*, University of Cambridge Department of Land Economy, Discussion Paper 14. It would have to be admitted that the available information on the state of disrepair of the total housing stock is deficient. A similar comment could be made about information on the scale of need in many other areas.
4. The figures, referring to 1985—1986, were reported in *New Society*, 5 December 1986.
5. See the report *Faith in the City* (1985).
6. This is the report by the National Federation of Housing Associations (1985). See also Cowie *et al.* (1984).
7. This survey is reported in Wicks (1978).
8. This imperfection in the capital market is a classic example of market failure which implies the need for public intervention.
9. These figures come from Hillman and Bollard (1985).
10. As reported by Jeremy Laurance in the article 'Frozen to Death' in *New Society*, 16 January 1987.
11. This paragraph draws on Hillman and Bollard (1985).
12. European Commission (1986).
13. Hillman and Bollard (1985).
14. Audit Commission (1986d) 'Making A Reality of Community Care'.
15. Audit Commission (1987).
16. We might note that Sheffield Council already uses MSC money to fund

the first year of employment of individuals in some social services, but then uses its own money to carry on employment beyond this point.
17. This is not, then, simply a plea for more money for the public sector. The finance and organisation of many public services need overhaul for additional resources to be well-spent.
18. Mays and Bevan (1987).
19. Hardman Report (1973) *The Dispersal of Government Work from London*, Cmnd. 5322, HMSO.

12

The Reform of Education and Training

'The level of staying on voluntarily beyond 16 has gone up substantially. I wish I could tell you that's because we've convinced them of the value of education, but I think really it's more to do with job prospects and unemployment. The kids have rumbled us. We'd say work harder, pass your exams and this will help you get a better job. That's now a load of codswallop. There are many decent young men and women who've made a decent job at school who've found there's nothing. Now that's bound to take its toll.'[1]

Introduction

It would have to be admitted that the government which came to power in 1979 had no clear strategy for education (and certainly not for training) beyond a vague promise to raise standards and a clearer commitment to reduce public expenditure. Successive Education Secretaries have groped their way towards some conception of *what* they might like to do but, in common with Education Secretaries for decades, have remained almost blind to *how* they might actually go about it. Meanwhile, the Employment Secretary has been able to use the Trojan Horse of the Manpower Services Commission to alter substantially the provision of education and training for the 14—19 age group.

Of course, in Chapter 7 we emphasised that the growth of the MSC has been a reaction to unforeseen circumstances rather than a part of any planned strategy. Just as the Community Programme was constituted in a hurry to respond to burgeoning long-term unemployment, so the Youth Training Scheme and the expansion of its predecessor, the Youth Opportunities Programme, were panic responses to a politically worrying upsurge in school leaver unemployment between 1980 and 1982.

Thus we have the growing responsibilities of the MSC as the 'Ministers' Social Conscience'. The division of responsibility between the Departments of Education and Employment/MSC reflects the 150-year British tradition of dividing education and training into separate compartments, a division which nearly all those active in the field consider illogical and counterproductive. Aside from this interdepartmental rivalry we also have the problem of the civil war between Whitehall and local government which, as we have seen, has proved so damaging in the fields of housing, social services and so on. Yet, as we shall try to demonstrate, there is and has been for a long time a clear recognition of the deficiencies of our education system and our training record and of the reforms required to remedy them. All that is lacking is the political will to generate the necessary consensus and momentum for change.

The Problem

... our deficiency is not merely a deficiency in technical education, but in general intelligence, and unless we remedy this want we shall gradually but surely find that our undeniable superiority in wealth and perhaps in energy will not save us from decline.[2]

A survey of a representative sample of 45 small and medium-sized manufacturing firms in West Germany and Britain, conducted in 1984, revealed that the German plants had on average 63 per cent higher labour productivity than the British firms.[3] This could not be accounted for by differences in scale or in the age of the machinery. The only significant distinguishing characteristic between the British and German firms was in the quality of the workforce, from top to bottom. The production manager in the British firm usually had a sales or financial background or had learned on the job, while the German production manager was usually a graduate engineer. The average British foreman had risen from the shop floor and had no formal qualifications beyond an apprenticeship. His German counterparts were trained craftsmen who, in addition, had obtained the higher qualification of 'Meister', involving not only technical skills but also proficiency in staff supervision and work organisation. Even shop floor workers in West Germany were trained to higher standards and had a greater competency in the operation of machinery.

Further comparisons of the education system in Britain, France, West Germany and Japan reveal a consistent pattern, especially in the field of mathematical skills which might be expected to be closely correlated to achievement at work.[4] The best of the British at school-leaving age have mastered mathematical skills which can match, if not clearly surpass, the achievements of foreign students. However, the attainments of the average and below-average British pupils were drastically below those achieved in West Germany, Japan and France. This appears to be a reflection of the continuing dominance of the British secondary school curriculum by the requirements of university entrance, where the stress is placed on over-specialisation at an early age, and the intensive training of an intellectual elite which gives Britain the greatest number of Nobel prizes per head of population in the world, but also leads to economic failure because of the inattention to providing the broad mass of young people with a stimulating curriculum and relevant qualifications. This is the *crème de la crème* syndrome of British education.

Approximately 40 per cent of British school leavers have traditionally entered the labour market without qualifications and sound survey evidence suggests that one in eight of a sample of British people born in 1958 today have severe problems in basic numeracy and literacy.[5] We can add to this the evidence we accumulated in Chapter 3 that well over half of those who have been out of work for over one year have no qualifications and that nearly one in four had problems with basic numeracy and literacy. We also noted that the market for unskilled labour is shrinking while the demand for well qualified and flexible people grows. When we link together a badly educated and trained adult workforce and poor labour productivity, a continuing output of unqualified children from a troubled education system and the problem of youth unemployment and a very large number of unskilled and poorly educated long-term unemployed, we can see why the education and training system is under scrutiny.

It is not clear to this author why this remains a party political football, however. Sophisticated statistical analyses of the performance of education authorities in England, which adjust for differences in the social and economic background of pupils, find that poorly performing authorities include Brent and Haringey, but also Norfolk, Bedfordshire, Essex and Bromley, and the best performing authorities include Harrow and Barnet, but also Liverpool, Manchester, Newcastle and indeed Cleveland which scores ninth out of ninety-six authorities.[6] There is no correlation between educational performance and the political parentage of authorities. Within one local authority schools with the same social mix of pupils can nevertheless differ strongly in their educational performance, as was shown in one especially influential study.[7] The best state schools and the best authorities are superlative, but the worst can be very poor indeed. It is surely in the interests of everyone, whatever their politics, to understand the reasons for this diversity more clearly and to bring the standards of poorer schools and authorities up to the high standards of the best.

Those who have followed the education and training debate since the 1960s talk about an incredible feeling of *déjà vu* and indeed the quote with which I began this section comes from the Schools Enquiry Royal Commission of *1868*. A veteran of the Victorian Royal Commissions on various aspects of the education question (and there were many such Commissions, whose radical recommendations were watered down or just ignored) would find himself completely at home in the debates of the 1980s. It is as if we have known precisely what is wrong for over 120 years but have failed miserably to implement reforms. To understand the mess that education and training is in now we must answer the question: why has 120 years of sound advice on education reform not been enacted?

Certainly one cannot fail to be astonished at the list of criticisms unearthed by the Royal Commissions and Reports from 1861 to 1945.[8] The first in the series, the Newcastle Commission, worried about too many children leaving school without learning to read properly.[9] The Clarendon Commission in 1864 criticised the narrow curriculum of the top public schools with the overwhelming emphasis on classics and religion in the tradition of Thomas Arnold.[10] Royal Commissions in 1875 and 1884 noted the far superior technical education available on the Continent and remarked on how little regard had been paid to the recommendations of the previous Commissions.[11] The Balfour Committee repeated everything in 1929, laying particular emphasis on the lack of demand from industry for people trained in science and engineering and the Hadow (1927) and Spens (1938) Reports criticised the lack of provision in secondary schools for non-academic children.[12] They all read like the most recent White Papers on Education, authored by Sir Keith Joseph and Kenneth Baker.

There is now well-documented argument that places the initial blame on this inertia on the very process of industrialisation in pre-Victorian Britain.[13] Our industrial revolution was 'voluntary' in the sense that the state played virtually no role, a pattern also true of the other Anglo-Saxon nations including of course the United States. But in this they were entirely exceptional, for in every other industrial nation, on the Continent and in Japan, industrialisation was force-fed by the state, which also recognised a need for a national education system as the natural partner to economic prosperity. The response of the elite in Britain to industrialisation was schizophrenic: at once welcoming Britain's industrial wealth as a source of military and imperial power (and a very nice life style) while despising the consequences of industrialism and urbanism and showing nothing short of contempt for manufacturers and businessmen. The narrowness of the curriculum and the elitism of British education, constructed in the Clarendon Public Schools, seem to have spread to Oxbridge, the Grammars, the Redbrick Universities and the Polytechnics. The fact that the switch to comprehensive schooling has neither improved nor worsened matters is precisely because the comprehensives have focused their attention on the academic education of the best of the ability range while neglecting to promote a curriculum relevant to the less able children.[14] The British tradition of concentrating educational resources on the brightest children lives on and produces an unbalanced system of schooling which mirrors and reinforces the imbalances in the labour market.

In the late nineteenth century, educational reform fell victim to a combination of complacency and diversions. Why worry about the parlous state of the machine tool industry in Britain, *vis-à-vis* Germany, when Britannia ruled the waves, we had the Empire and God was an Englishman? Even in economic terms in the 1880s we were still on top (with the United States) although it was clear others were catching up. In the post-war period we have been clearly surpassed by northern and central European countries, but most post-war prime ministers were more concerned with the future of battleships (Churchill), Nasser (Eden), playing uncle to a US President (Macmillan), playing with matchsticks (Home), playing politics (Wilson), or getting into Europe (Heath). Even the one post-war prime minister who was Education Secretary is more concerned with her role as international stateswoman.[15] It would take commitment and persistence to achieve educational reform and the returns flow over some decades; the dramatic foreign policy gesture helps win this year's election.

When Sweden's education system went comprehensive there was a conscious attempt to create a cross-party political consensus, and curriculum reform was discussed alongside organisational change.[16] The contrast with Britain is embarrassing, with the refusal to recognise that educational reform above all requires continuity and consensus. It seems obvious that one cannot change the education system without first earning the support of the teaching profession and, because educational reform (like all reform) is a process and not an event, which takes decades to yield results, there is a need for cross-party consensus. But politicians of all parties prefer to score cheap party political points and refuse to recognise (as we will argue below) that there is in fact something of a consensus already in existence about how to reform the system. Education in the 1980s is the case study on how not to approach change, for change without consent promotes conflict and in this case has created a demoralised, disillusioned and cynical teaching profession.

Indeed, talking to the teachers with twenty years or more in the profession, who had never been in trade unions until recently, it is so quite simply sad to see how far things have gone. The quote at the beginning of this chapter also hints at the consequences of poor employment prospects for the motivation of the children. How can you build a dynamic economy on the base of an education system where the teachers are tired of ministerial contempt and the children wonder what the system offers them anyway?

The Response

The Youth Training Scheme

YTS was introduced in 1983 from a blueprint that had been accepted by the MSC only in the previous summer and by 1986 had been transformed into a two-year scheme designed to provide a 'permanent bridge between school and work'. It superseded the earlier Youth Opportunities Programme, inherited from the last Labour administration, which had been designed to cope with rising unemployment among the young; YTS suffers from being similarly labelled a makework scheme rather than a permanent contribution to Britain's training effort.

If we look carefully at the school leavers who enter the YTS and at their reasons for doing so, the impression comes across strongly that the scheme is still regarded as a second-best option for those unable to go on to higher education or into ordinary employment.[17] At age 16, young people face four broad options: the best qualified stay on for higher and further education; the next best qualified go into conventional employment; the less qualified go into the YTS; and the least qualified school leavers often reject all of these options and enter unemployment. Six out of ten of those joining the YTS in Scotland said that they did so because they could not find a job, rather than because of the intrinsic merits of the scheme. It is also clear that many employers remain ambivalent about the scheme and still appear more impressed by traditional academic school qualifications than achievement on the YTS.

Just as there is considerable diversity in the quality of schools, so there is diversity in the quality of YTS places. The best YTS schemes, often run by big firms of good reputation such as ICI, offer well thought-out training and attempt to place the majority of their participants in full-time employment or further training at the end of the scheme. These well-run schemes are considerably over-subscribed by young people (especially the ICI scheme in Cleveland). By 1986 the MSC was claiming that 85 per cent of schemes were satisfactory by their own definition and three out of four trainees in Scotland considered their own schemes well run.[18] The remaining problems are four-fold: a minority of schemes remain unsatisfactory; the majority of young people who go into conventional employment receive little or no further training; the YTS is still perceived as a second-best option; and a minority of school leavers refuse to enter the scheme.

If we look at this last group it is clear that these youngsters have the worst (and often no) qualifications of all school leavers and emerge as a 'small, hard core of alienated, unemployed refusers'.[19] One can speculate that these are the young people who would spend much of their fourth and fifth years of secondary education playing truant. If they feel let down by their state schools it is not surprising that they are also alienated from a state-run training scheme which they perceive, however inaccurately, to be exploitative. The answer would seem to lie in better schools with a relevant curriculum which would give the youngsters an incentive to gain qualifications rather than force them on to a scheme which they perceive as a waste of time, by abolishing their right to supplementary benefit. We are putting the onus on incentives for schools, colleges and employers to offer relevant courses and training rather than incentives for individuals to force them to do things against their will. If the law could not force them to stay at school when they were 14, the abolition of benefit would probably not force them on to a training scheme at age 16. Instead they might find an alternative, and illegal, source of income.

The number of unsatisfactory schemes has fallen over the last three years as the MSC has built up skills in evaluating the managing agents and this improvement has occurred simultaneously with the expansion of the scheme to two years. The last follow-up survey for YTS leavers in 1985 showed 59 per cent in employment, 14 per cent on another YTS, and 26 per cent unemployed, but this was a significant improvement on earlier surveys.[20] However, the success of YTS in placing young people in employment varies regionally, as one would expect, with 90 per cent or more of participants in some labour markets in the South-East finding jobs on leaving the scheme, compared with less than 40 per cent in Cleveland. There is also a dramatic difference between the sexes, with females in Cleveland more than twice as likely as males to find work.[21] The better placing rates for the YTS in the last couple of years might simply reflect an improving balance of supply and demand in the teenage labour market, with the ending of the 1960s baby boom coinciding with an upturn in demand for teenagers, especially women. Given that the YTS is still perceived as second-best to an ordinary job, there are signs that the scheme might struggle in its recruitment as the ordinary job market recovers from the parlous state of the early 1980s.

One of the more unsatisfactory aspects of the youth labour market is the considerable number of youngsters who enter conventional employment without much in the way of further training. Among young people who left school in 1984 and were in jobs in the spring of 1986, nearly half were receiving no training while only one quarter were receiving training of more than two years' duration.[22] The contrast with the youth labour market in West Germany is quite embarrassing. It is illegal in West Germany to employ people under 18 except as part of their dual-based system of vocational education and training, with the requirement on employers for day-release. The system is organised and financed by the employers through the powerful local Chambers of Commerce which also have trade-union participation. The employers do not have to be offered compulsion or financial incentives to organise a system which they know they will benefit from as a long-term investment in the skills of the workforce. This brings us to the attitudes of employers in Britain *vis-à-vis* the value of training as a whole.

Adult Training - The Cinderella Service

> The vast majority of companies, in spite of initial claims to the contrary, were not very interested in training and had an attitude which bordered on complacency.[23]

This was the conclusion of an official report into the attitudes of British companies towards training. The punchline was that most firms saw training as an overhead to be cut in bad times rather than as an investment in long-run competitiveness and profitability, as could be witnessed by the severe collapse in traditional apprenticeships in industry in the 1979–82 recession. The report estimated that British firms spent on average 0.15 per cent of turnover on training their workforce which, on available data, compares badly with overseas competitors. What information we have suggests that the average British worker gets 16 hours off-the-job training a year compared with a *minimum* of 40 hours in West Germany. There are numerous case studies which suggest a strong relationship between business performance and a strong commitment to training. The 'best' firms can spend over 3 per cent of turnover on training (IBM) and one can find firms in the UK where training receives the serious attention it deserves (ICI).

The response of industry to this report was, in general, dismissive. British employers, in common with other British institutions, have an Acquired Immune Defensive Syndrome which allows them to blame all other institutions for their problems while being entirely unresponsive to outside or indeed self-criticism (Westminster is in fact an extreme example of the syndrome). Debates on training do not attract the majority of employers in need of encouragement, but the already converted few who take training seriously. Why? It is probably not so much complacency, as ignorance of all the basic lessons of good management. If one reads the new 'bibles' of management which have been produced in the last few years one is immediately struck by how many of the recommendations seem to state what ought to be plainly obvious.[24] Apparently the keys to business success include clear leadership, the decentralisation of decision making, a system of close financial controls, specific attention to products and customers, the motivation of employees through close communication and appropriate incentives and recognition of the importance of innovation and training. The very fact that all these things have to be explicitly pointed out is an indication of the problem of British management's inadequacies. It would also be germane to add that too few trade unions pay close attention to training as an issue for collective bargaining.

Aside from an exhortation that firms ought to do better (which, like most exhortations seems to have no effect), the response of the government is the MSC's Adult Training Strategy (ATS) which, in 1986–87, made available some £250 million to help 250,000 adults through a confusing plethora of courses in colleges of further education, skill centres or in employer-based training. This was less than 10 per cent of the MSC employment and training budget to help about 1 per cent of the employed labour force. It is not clear, however, that even this meagre provision was well targeted. The National Audit Office has criticised the MSC for its lack of knowledge of the balance of supply and demand in local labour markets, its failure to assess and evaluate adequately its various programmes, its failure to investigate precisely what training local employers *do* carry out, and the paucity of knowledge about the skills, or lack of them, amongst the British labour force, in and out of work.[25] It is not clear whether the training which is provided is relevant or is merely adding to skills already in excess supply and, given that there is no system of national training standards, participants can never be sure that if they receive a certificate it actually means anything. To sum up, the MSC is largely stabbing in the dark.

The Future

It is useful to report briefly on five new initiatives which have been tried in recent years or will be the subject of pilot studies in the near future.

Firstly, we have the government plan for up to twenty City Technology Colleges, a kind of resurrected technical school, to be set up around the country (including one in Middlesbrough). These schools are part of the general aim to bias the schools curriculum away from its traditional academic base and to inculcate a more technological orientation. This aim is uncontroversial, but is the chosen instrument a wise one? We have tried to stress that one of the problems of Britain's education system is that it trains an elite intensively while neglecting the average and below-average student. The first worry is that a few isolated colleges will surely perpetuate this tradition by giving a minority a very good technical education but failing to raise standards in *all* our schools. This is especially likely to prove the case if the colleges cream off the best pupils and the best teachers, leaving the remaining schools inadequately staffed to deal with the pupils of less aptitude. It is not necessarily the case that we need ten thousand more 'elite artisans' but rather an output of reasonably well-educated children from all our schools. This viewpoint seems to be reflected by private firms who, rather than placing large amounts of money in individual schools, seem to prefer to spread their resources and construct on-going relationships with a wide range of local schools.

The City Technology Colleges epitomise the 'top−down' approach to educational reform: initiatives are planned in Whitehall and then imposed, whether or not a consensus for such change has been generated. By contrast the experiments in decentralised budgeting, where individual schools and their headmasters are given greater control over expenditure, have exemplified the alternative 'bottom—up' approach. After three years of piloting the idea, the local education authority in Cambridgeshire was able to generalise the approach to other schools by consent.[26] All three political groups on the council either enthusiastically support, or at least do not oppose, the idea. Of course the pilots have thrown up difficult questions, especially about the need for in-service training in management skills for head and senior teachers, but the approach to the answers to these questions is consciously cooperational. However, the government has now hastily decided to *impose* decentralised budgeting on all local authorities, instead of allowing for further pilot studies elsewhere in Britain, to see if this approach can be generalised.

In early 1987 we had a further example, of potentially far-reaching influence, of 'bottom—up' reform. The London Compact involves a number of the city's employers guaranteeing future employment and training to young people, providing they perform well in their last two years in school, achieving a record for punctuality and good work. It amounts to a future employer—future employee development contract which puts obligations on both partners. The arrangement is being developed by the much-maligned Inner London Education Authority and is specifically targeted at disadvantaged schools in Hackney and Tower Hamlets. It is not clear why the public sector (with the exception of the Armed Forces cadetship schemes) as a whole does not also launch its own pilots along these lines, with each local authority and public body required to experiment with some form of Compact, aimed precisely at those young people who find conventional schooling irrelevant and the YTS unattractive. It copes precisely with the problem of children giving up in school because they do not think they have much of a future anyway, by giving them an incentive to participate in the system.

Another recent innovation is the Technical and Vocational Education Initiative (TVEI) which was planned by the MSC as a way of countering the anti-vocational bias of the traditional curriculum.[27] This initiative is most interesting because of its experimentation with the 'modular' approach to the curriculum and the use of continuous assessment. Participants take a series of modules of varying lenths in a diverse range of subjects - a few weeks of work experience, a couple of months of information technology, and so on. The modular approach has also found its way into the YTS and the Job Training Scheme (see below). The TVEI ran into some problems, however: the courses were sometimes not well integrated with the remainder of the traditional curriculum, on occasion they encouraged specialisation at too early an age (a traditional failing in British education), and the most able students still tended to opt for the examinations geared to university entrance. There is also the problem that there is no national system of certification, so it is still not quite clear what a TVEI qualification means. Finally, the experience of TVEI pointed to a shortage of teachers with suitable skills, shortages of appropriate materials and premises, and the need for improved in-service teacher training. It also has to be acknowledged that industry was often less willing to involve itself in curriculum development than had been hoped, and usually only those schools and authorities which had a fairly long history of business co-operation had comprehensively planned the involvement of businesses in TVEI.

The controversial Job Training Scheme was extended nationally in early 1987, after a very short pilot period in ten areas, including Billingham in Cleveland. At the time of writing, no proper evaluations have been conducted so that we have no real means of passing judgement on the scheme. From what we know so far the quality of training offered is not very high, but it is interesting to note that the MSC would like to promote a modular approach, mixing on- and off- the-job training in a flexible package lasting between three and twelve months. It could therefore provide the precursor for the kind of adult training programme for the long-term unemployed which we have tried to outline below. However, it is not clear whether the government will provide enough additional resources to fund worthwhile training or will simply cut existing training programmes to finance the JTS; the allowance paid under the scheme appears unreasonably low. In November 1987 the government decided to merge JTS with the Community Programme (Chapter 7) after it became clear that the scheme was failing to attract sufficient participants.

The Unacknowledged Consensus

One of the key features of the West German education and training system is that there appears to be a widespread consensus on what the system is for, how it should be organised, and how it should be financed.[28] In West Germany and Japan teaching is a well-paid, respected profession with high social status. If we were to realise that British schooling is fighting a series of ideological ghosts, it would be possible to acknowledge the wide degree of consensus which already exists over how to reform the system in this country.

The 'socialist' purports to believe in 'equality': the education and training system exists to give the best chances to those disadvantaged by their social and economic background. The 'liberal' believes in educating the individual in the values necessary to promote a tolerant society. The 'conservative' worries about standards and the need to have a system geared to providing individuals who can deliver economic prosperity, as entrepreneurs or skilled workers. But are these philosophies really mutually exclusive? Consider the problem of the large minority of under-achievers who leave school with no qualifications, receive an inadequate training with employers, and end up competing for the shrinking number of unskilled jobs. If educational reform could significantly improve the qualifications of this group by providing a curriculum and style of instruction relevant enough to provide such young people with incentives to perform, we would be raising the average standard of the workforce and this should feed through to improved economic performance (to please the 'conservatives'), while a more prosperous and equal society is also likely to be a more tolerant one (for the 'liberals').

Alternatively, consider that one of the most important of human qualities is the ability to communicate with other people and work with them as a team. This is equally true for the competitive success of an individual firm, for the success of families and communities, and for constructing a tolerant and decent society. What Britain needs to learn is how to achieve the right balance between competition and co-operation: that is, fierce competition *between* firms to spur product and process innovation,[29] and co-operation *within* each firm to build an efficient, winning team. So, to teach teamwork at school should please 'conservatives' who want healthy firms, 'socialists' who believe in fraternity, and 'liberals' who want tolerance.

To return to practical matters, what evidence can we offer to convince the reader that there really is an unacknowledged consensus in education and youth training? All three main political parties, and most education professionals, now agree on the need for a nationally-defined, broadly-based, core curriculum which would aim for the attainment by *all* students of certain minimum standards in a wide range of subjects. This curriculum would be set after full consultation with a wide variety of interests but should not impose detailed syllabuses and specific teaching methods. It would have a more explicitly practical bias to counter the traditional academic structure of education, and would de-emphasise the importance of formal examinations. Instead, realistic individual learning targets would be set, so avoiding mechanistic learning aimed solely at passing exams rather than developing the individual's skills. It would be simply copying what is already standard practice in West Germany, France and Japan. There is also agreement on the need to resurrect the status of the teaching profession, to provide better in-service teacher training, and to allow for more late entry into the profession so that teachers can gain experience of other varied forms of work before they embark on actual teaching.

More radically, there is a widespread feeling that the whole system of education and training for teenagers (14–19) needs an overhaul.[30] It has been suggested that the GCSE, YTS, 'A' levels and a profusion of other courses should be fused into a comprehensive scheme of education, training and work experience for this age group. Students would build up a series of modules of education, vocational training, work experience with employers, community work, and so on, which could be carried out at secondary schools, further education or tertiary colleges, on employers' premises or with voluntary organisations. The result would be the gradual building up of a profile of achievement which at the age of 18 or 19 could be used to gain access to work or higher education. Pupils could switch from school to another institution at age 14 if they so wished and teachers would be eligible to work at any of these educational institutions. At the age of 16 a taxable grant would be payable to all at an equal rate, whether the individual chose mainly college or employer-based education and training.[31] It would be illegal to employ anyone under 18, as in West Germany, without participating in this scheme with its requirement for day-release.

Such a scheme presents an obvious set of advantages. We would overcome the perception of YTS as a second-best scheme by treating trainees and their more 'academic' counterparts as equals. Access to higher education would be available to all, not just those presently taking 'A' levels. Students could choose to build up an adequate profile of achievement on the basis of employer- or voluntary-based work experience, vocational training, and continued study of English and mathematics. Students would not be forced onto state benefits or prematurely into work because they need to supplement the family income.[32] The whole system would be the responsibility of a Department of Education and Training working through a (reformed) structure of local government. Most of the worthwhile initiatives outlined earlier — decentralised budgeting, the modular and continuous assessment approach of TVEI, the Compact — would be easily integrated into this general structure. Indeed, one of its strengths would be to combine a national strategy with as much local experimentation and diversity as was feasible. The Education and Training Inspectorates would be merged to provide a mechanism for evaluation and the diffusion of the best practices.

As for post-18 higher education, this is a whole subject in itself, but the important principle is that the universities and polytechnics would be required to adapt *themselves* to this new structure of schooling, rather than schooling being required to structure *itself* around the requirements of university entrance. The key issue is one of access: that the institutions of higher education be required to open their doors to the non-academic, the mature and the disadvantaged student rather than only to the traditional 'A' level stream.[33]

The overall philosophy is one of 'community schooling' whereby education (widely defined) is based in individual communities, involving all sections of the community, relevant to the problems and the potential of those communities and targeted quite specifically at the less advantaged people in those communities. This philosophy would embrace the idea of encouraging *all* parents, not just the cliques who dominate governing bodies, to participate in the school.

Adult Training and the Long-term Unemployed

What we have discussed so far is mainly relevant to todays generation of teenagers in the hope that we can turn out a more productive, a more tolerant and a more equal generation of young adults. This is prevention rather than cure: avoiding economic and social problems like long-term unemployment by building a base for preventing its emergence in the first place. But what about the existing adult workforce, both in and out of work?

There is a growing consensus that adult training will only obtain more resources in the context of a levy—grant system of financing training.[34] The MSC would gather information on the proportion of turnover spent on average on adult training in each industry and would then set annual targets for increasing this average. Firms which spent more than the average would receive a grant from the government to cover the difference, but firms which spent less than the average would pay a levy equal to the difference. In effect, firms which paid the least attention to training would be subsidising the firms which devoted the most attention. Over several years the proportion of turnover devoted to training would be increased in all British firms. The first step would be to make it a statutory requirement for all firms to report on what training they carry out, and for the MSC to carry out training audits and disseminate the results, emphasising the best practice in progressive firms. Those firms willing to enter into development contracts along the lines suggested in Chapter 10 (and including an agreed training programme) would be the only firms exempted from the levy–grant.

However, this still leaves us with a large core of ill-qualified, poorly skilled and educated long-term unemployed whom firms are reluctant to hire, even when offered a generous subsidy to do so. Clearly, a grant–levy system is relevant only to the existing workforce — how do the long-term unemployed 'get in on the act'? It has to be admitted that there is, as yet, no consensus on how to deal with this most difficult of questions, for the simple reason that few people have yet addressed themselves seriously to it.[35] The plight of the unemployed school leaver and the condition of our education system quite correctly attract attention, but unfortunately there seems to be less thought left over for the problems and needs of the older, long-term unemployed.

The proposed ideas outlined here are necessarily tentative, but follow on from our discussion of the most interesting new initiatives of recent years. What we would suggest is adapting the modular approach pioneered in education to the needs of the disadvantaged long-term unemployed. The MSC would gather information about their existing skills and needs and then, for each individual, design a development programme which would consist of modules of adult education in basic skills or new technologies (in the same further education and tertiary colleges catering for teenagers), vocational training or re-training in skill centres or with employers, and community work with those voluntary organisations most skilled in dealing with the educationally disadvantaged. At the end the adult might be presented with the same kind of profile of achievement as the teenager (with the same chance of access to higher education?). A marginal employment subsidy could then be used to place the adult with a normal employer. The employer would have a double inducement to recruit: a subsidy *and* a proven record of skills, training and work experience.

It should be noted that we already have some experience of programmes aimed at disadvantaged young people — the Community Industry Scheme and Mode BI YTS. These schemes often utilise the skills of voluntary organisations with experience in dealing with particularly disadvantaged teenagers, but they are very much on the margins of the MSC's work, and mode BI YTS is considerably more expensive than YTS placements with conventional employers. A second point to make is that job centres cannot expect the long-term unemployed to volunteer: the staff must go out and actively recruit, perhaps building on the experience of welfare rights activists who try to help people claim the social benefits to which they are entitled.

Would it not be possible to extend the concept of the employer–student compact described earlier, to the long-term unemployed? Firms would offer permanent employment to an adult on the condition that he fulfill a development programme involving basic skills training, and so on, and a period of work experience with the firm. Perhaps, if a few enlightened employers and public-sector bodies tried pilots along these lines, we would learn more about the best ways to help and the best practices might spread?

This leads on to exploiting the evidence from Cambridgeshire on the potentially beneficial impact of decentralised budgeting. We are suggesting that the MSC concentrate solely on its role as a labour board, running the job centres, building up information on the skills and needs of the unemployed (extending Restart), building an intelligence base on the skill requirements of local labour markets and the existing training provision by local employers, and co-ordinating adult training and education. However, we should allow for a significant degree of decentralisation, deliberately encouraging local MSC management to experiment with different options, utilising whichever local organisations are relevant. For example, in some areas it might be possible to get the local Chamber of Commerce to administer schemes of employer-based adult training and the capacity to draw on voluntary organisations for help is likely to vary from locality to locality. We are suggesting that some MSC areas be given devolved responsibility for budgeting on a pilot basis so that they may plan the kind of Adult Training Strategy most appropriate to the communities they are serving.

The role of re-integrating the long-term unemployed into the world of work and learning is a momentous task in itself. If the local managerial talent of the MSC (and there is a considerable amount available) were focused on this one objective, it would be likely to prove more advantageous than dissipating that talent by asking the MSC to do so much else besides. It would put the focus on MSC as 'Management Skills under Crisis', and suggests that there may be an administrative version of the economist's Tinbergen rule: if you aim one agency at several targets you may end up missing them all; it is probably better for one agency to concentrate on one task only.

Notes

1. A local government official in Cleveland quoted in Foord *et al.* (1985), p. 59.
2. From the 1868 Schools Enquiry Royal Commission, quoted in Barnett (1986).
3. A pilot inquiry conducted by A. Daly, D. Hitchens and K. Wagner, in the *National Institute Economic Review*, February 1985.
4. The National Institute, under the direction of S.J. Prais, has now built up a series of studies comparing British schooling and vocational training with West Germany's (*National Institute Economic Review*, August 1983 and May 1985), France's (May 1986) and Japan's (February 1987). There is also a chapter by Prais in Worswick (1985) which in addition contains a chapter by R. Russell on the West German vocational training scheme, and an excellent chapter by S. Maclure on the responsiveness of the British education system to change.
5. This refers to the National Child Development Study which follows the history of over 12,000 people born in the first week of March 1958. Today, nearly 13 per cent report trouble in reading, writing or arithmetic.
6. We refer here to the Sheffield University league table which adjusts local authorities' examination performance for differences in the socio-economic background of pupils using measures such as the proportion of children from professional or manual families, ethnic minorities, and so on. The results are well summarised in a chapter by J. Gray and D. Jesson in A. Harrison and J. Gretton (1987).
7. This is the famous study by M. Rutter *et al.* (1979).
8. A chapter by C. Barnett in Derek Morris (1985) lists fourteen reports between 1861 and 1945 in its bibliography.
9. Report of the Royal Commission on the State of Popular Education in England (2794, 1861).
10. Report of the Royal Commission on the Revenues and Management of certain Colleges and Schools, and the studies pursued and instruction given therein (3288, 1864).
11. Report of the Royal Commission on Scientific Instruction and the Advancement of Science (3981, 1872−75) and the Report of the Royal Commission on Technical Instruction (3981, 1884).
12. Report of the Committee of Inquiry into the Relationship of Technical Education to Other Forms of Education and to Industry and Commerce (1927). Report of the Consultative Committee of the Board of Education of the Adolescent (HMSO, 1927). The Hadow Report. Report of the Consultative Committee of the Board of Education on Secondary Education with Special Reference to Grammar Schools and Technical High Schools (HMSO, 1938). The Spens Report.
13. This thesis is well set out in the chapter by Barnett referred to in note 8 and in Barnett (1986). See also Dahrendorff (1982) and Wiener (1981).
14. This is well argued in Reynolds and Sullivan (1987).

15. The United States has suffered from the same problem of presidents pre-
occupied elsewhere. The only one to have taken educational reform
seriously (Johnson) was destroyed by the war in South-East Asia.
16. I owe this observation to Brian Abel-Smith.
17. This section on the YTS draws heavily on David Raffe's chapter in
A. Harrison and J. Gretton (1987).
18. Raffe, as referred to in note 17.
19. See notes 17 and 18.
20. This survey is reported in the *MSC Quarterly Report*, June 1986.
21. This information comes from the Cleveland Careers Service.
22. *MSC Quarterly Report*, February 1987.
23. From *A Challenge to Complacency*, a Coopers and Lybrand report for the
MSC and NEDO.
24. See, for example, the CBI report *Managing for Success* (1985) or the
celebrated *The Winning Streak* by Walter Goldsmith and David Clutterbuck
(1984). Interestingly, many of the companies looked at by Goldsmith and
Clutterbuck have recently performed very poorly and been victims of
takeover bids.
25. Department of Employment and Manpower Services Commission (1987)
Adult Training Strategy, National Audit Office, HMSO.
26. See chapter by T. Burgess in A. Harrison and J. Gretton (1987).
27. This section draws on the 1985 report by HM Inspectors, *The Technical
and Vocational Education Initiative: Early Developments*.
28. This stress on consensus is reported in a 1986 study by HM Inspectors which,
curiously, was the first time the Inspectorate had looked at overseas
examples.
29. Fierce competition in domestic markets is a distinguishing characteristic
of the Japanese economy.
30. This section closely follows the strategy for reform outlined by the National
Association of Head Teachers in 1987.
31. Such a grant is a feature of Labour and Alliance proposals.
32. The effect of inadequate financial provision for 16–18-year olds to continue in higher education is analysed by Burghes and Stagles (1983).
33. The best summary of these issues is contained in *Towards a Partnership*
published by the Council for Industry and Higher Education (1987) which
draws on the leaders of both business and academia.
34. The theoretical case for the levy–grant system is made in Metcalf (1986).
This proposal is Labour and Alliance policy and has been endorsed by the
Commons Select Committee on Employment.
35. I only came around to thinking seriously about the problem six months after
I began this study.

13

The Politics of Balanced Recovery

'It is not charity when the powerful help the poor ... it is justice.'[1]

Economists are not usually supposed to stray into the area of political or institutional reform. English higher reducation is rigidly segmented and each subject department is traditionally required to stick to its own patch. However, in the last few chapters we have suggested a series of policy initiatives which rely for their success on certain reforms to the way in which Britain is governed. The theme of this book has been that there are a large number of communities and people living in them who are being by-passed by the prosperity from which the majority of us are benefiting. Existing government initiatives are only scratching the surface of the problem and we have suggested that one of the reasons for this is that the unemployed and other disadvantaged groups have no real input into the solutions which are being discussed for their problems.

To a certain extent the unbalanced recovery is a mirror image of the imbalances in our top-heavy democracy. Far from reducing the powers of the state as part of a bid to 'destroy socialism', the present administration is enhancing the power of Whitehall, especially its capacity to override local government. In Chapter 6 we described the Urban Development Corporations, the government's chief weapon for inner city renewal, as 'socialist planning institutions', with tremendous powers over private property. The Education Bill which may become law in 1988 will allow schools to contract out of local authority control and become directly funded from Whitehall. Have many people thought through the implications of these changes, that a future left-of-centre government is being awarded a set of precedents which will allow it to extend state control far more effectively than Labour governments could in the 1960s or 1970s, because they were constrained by the constitutional safeguards offered by local councils? Suppose that all the remaining grammar schools opted to become centrally funded and that in the 1990s a new administration decided to close them all. It would then be the easiest thing to do because they would be directly financed from Whitehall.

The local authorities have not only performed the traditional role of a buffer between central government and local communities, the councils also act as an economist's 'automatic stabiliser'. If an administration in Whitehall decides to launch an irresponsible inflationary boom or an equally damaging deflation, this can at least be partly offset if local government does not join in. But there are dangers when a single institution controls all the financial levers and can lurch an entire nation in one direction or another. In the United States the attempt of one administration to destroy the tax base and eviscerate the social services can be partially offset by responsible state and local government. It is not clear that in the United Kingdom we have anything approaching the same kinds of checks and balances on the central state.

Some people might argue that it is important to have a strong central administrative apparatus to shift a nation onto a different course. I suspect that this is to misread how a modern and mature democracy works. If it functions at all it is on the basis of consent, with the governors required to go out and persuade the governed that a particular course of action is required for the benefit of the nation as a whole. Our present system gives the politicians at Westminster the illusion of absolute power, but they usually cannot wield it without promoting division or conflict and there are no clear incentives in our system for politicians to appeal to a majority. In 1983, and again in 1987, an administration could gain a big absolute majority of seats in the House of Commons on the basis of 43 per cent of the popular vote. Moroever, our unbalanced recovery seems to have its mirror image in regional voting patterns, with 63 per cent of the electorate in the North of England, 70 per cent of the Welsh and 75 per cent of the Scottish voters rejecting the Conservative administration in 1987. Never mind, Westminster can in theory override this imbalance in the political map just as the majority of affluent people in Britain can ignore the less fortunate, if they believe in the realities of power politics and ignore their conscience.

In Chapter 11 we looked at a number of locally provided services and described the organisational and financial chaos which leads to the inefficient waste of resources, while the problems of bad housing and inadequate social services persist. We suggested ways of reforming the delivery of these services to make them more relevant to the communities they serve and simultaneously tilt their recruitment towards those people who are the most disadvantaged in the labour market. These reforms presuppose the existence of competent local government and we have looked at some of the evidence gathered by the Audit Commission on this issue. What we would like to do is outline some of the reforms to the finance, organisation and structure of local councils which would make for effective, responsive and democratic local government.[2] The message of the Audit Commission, relayed here, is that, if local government sometimes fails to achieve high standards, the answer is to reform local government, not to supplant it with Whitehall control.

The Reform of Local Government

It should be apparent from the discussion in Chapters 9 and 11 that everybody's first priority is the reform of local government *finance*. The Audit Commission would like to see a much simplified system of distributing rate support grant, which would be aimed solely at equalising the level of resources available to local authorities so that the same standard of service could be provided in any part of the country regardless of how good the local tax base might be.[3] Such a simplification would also improve the fairness of the system, because its capricious features stem precisely from its complexity. Controls on local authorities' use of capital receipts would be scrapped and Whitehall would limit itself to controlling the overall level of new borrowing.

Nearly everybody who has looked at it in detail considers the government's proposals for a poll tax or community charge to be just plain daft. Domestic rates are a regressive tax, but one which is cheap to administer and very hard to avoid paying. The community charge will be significantly more regressive and far more difficult to collect, with the likelihood of considerable evasion. A more sensible reform would be to base a property tax on the capital value of a home, with the base revalued each time a house is sold.[4] This would get around the problem of re-valuing property to update the notional rateable value of a home. The local tax base would become less regressive, while remaining efficient. Rate support grant (and with it central control) could be reduced as a proportion of local expenditure and replaced by a local income tax and/or charges for property services. Non-domestic rates on commercial property could be levied uniformly, collected nationally and passed back to local authorities as a part of the rate support grant. If a local authority wished to raise its expenditure it could do so only by increasing domestic rates and/or local income tax or charges. Local government would then be more accountable to the local electorate for its spending decisions.

If local authorities are corrupt or inefficient it is the job of the local electorate to do something about it — that's democracy. In 1982 the Labour Party won 51 out of 52 seats on Islington Borough Council in London with 52 per cent of the vote on a 40 per cent turnout. One seat went to the opposition which had gathered 48 per cent of the vote. That's not democracy! The case for electoral reform at the local level is as strong as it is for Westminster and ministers and the tabloid press ought not to harp on about 'loony councils' without appreciating that they are a consequence of a corrupt electoral system. The Audit Commission believes that requiring all councils to re-elect one-third of their members each year and providing better information to the electors on the perform-ance of their local authorities would also help to increase *accountability*.[5]

The *organisation* of local government is another area for reform. There are 26,000 councillors in Britain and the Audit Commission considers that this is too many. The result is the proliferation of 'management by committee' and local authorities ought to move to more of a 'Cabinet' style of government, with more delegation to senior officers and com-mittees confined to monitoring performance against agreed policies and priorities. The introduction of two-tier local authorities in the early 1970s was a mistake and it would be wise to move back to unitary authorities.[6] The effectiveness of a council like Sheffield's is very much a consequence of the reforms introduced in its internal structure and the fact that the authority covers the whole of the city. Sheffield has also helped to pioneer the decentralisation of local services to make them more relevant to the communitites which are being served. Local government would become responsible for setting priorities and standards, while securing the provision of services from private contractors, public agen-cies, voluntary groups and, increasingly, community organisations. The local authorities have more potential for learning to listen to the people they represent than a London-based bureaucracy.

Clearly any institutional reform only works if the actors in the system are honestly prepared to change too. The principle that we are trying to further is that all public-sector bodies have to become far more respon-sive to the needs and priorities of individual communities. Whitehall, or unelected bodies answerable only to Whitehall, should not be telling everybody how to run their lives in a mature, late-twentieth-century democracy. This is not simply a value judgement. The empirical evidence which we have assembled in Chapters 6 to 12 suggests that Whitehall and its 'quangos' are not listening to the communities which they are supposed to be helping, but imposing their own ideas. Surely we need to be stimulating discussion about what needs to be done to counter the unbalanced recovery at the level of individual communities? It needs to be stressed again that people have a right to 'own' their own problems and to have an input into developing the solutions to their problems.

The Role of the Manpower Services Commission

In Chapter 12 we argued that the MSC is being overloaded with the responsibility for administering too many different programmes. We also suggested that the division of responsibility for education and training between the Departments of Education and Employment/MSC was il-logical. Taking responsibility for the Youth Training Scheme away from the MSC and giving it to a reformed Department of Education and Train-ing would kill two birds with one stone. Many of the employment schemes run by the MSC such as the Community Programme should be integrated with normal local and health authority work. This would leave the MSC with the functions of a labour board, performing the twin role of gather-ing intelligence on the state of the labour market and sponsoring train-ing for adults. Some people might argue that this role, too, would be carried out best by local authorities, but it might be more sensible to reform local government first and then see how a reformed structure could cope with its existing roles and with the decentralisation of services to local communities.

The government's proposals for reforming the MSC make much less sense. The plan is to take the running of the job centres away from the Commission and hand it directly to the Department of Employment. The job centres would be fused with the unemployment benefit offices and the MSC would become a training and 'schemes' agency to be renamed the Training Commission. The idea of fusing benefit offices and job centres is a good one: not because we want to make sure that people claiming benefit are genuinely looking for work, but to ensure that the unemployed can get access to all the information they need about their entitlement to benefit. It makes sense for the unemployed individual to have to travel to only one office to claim benefit and engage in job search.

Also, an individual who is thinking of taking a low-paid job should have immediate access to information about the benefits he can claim, such as Family Income Supplement, which will raise his net income. The use of simple microcomputer technology should facilitate this service.

However, separating the job centres from the agency responsible for training seems less sensible. In the last chapter we saw that the National Audit Office was not very happy that the MSC's Adult Training Strategy was based on good intelligence on the skills of the unemployed and the requirements of employers. Now it is suggested that the intelligence and training functions should be entirely separated. But if the MSC does not have direct responsibility for gathering information on the skills and needs of the unemployed, how can it tailor its adult training to meet those needs?

This worry is compounded when one considers the suggestion made in government circles that employers should be encouraged not to report their vacancies to job centres, but should advertise available jobs through private agencies, journals and so on. This would seem to undermine the intelligence role completely and would mean that the MSC's training would be even more likely to be stabbing in the dark. The job centres would cater solely for the long-term unemployed who would only have access to places on the Community Programme, the various training schemes or the very low-paid, low-skilled jobs. The best employment opportunities would be confined to the specialised information networks to which the long-term unemployed simply do not have access. A better way to isolate and marginalise the long-term unemployed even further could not be imagined. Whoever is pushing this idea can have little knowledge of the actual operation of local labour markets. We have tried to argue that the long-term unemployed are already being by-passed by the normal channels in the labour market and this proposal would merely exacerbate the problem.

The government would also like to increase the employers' representation on the MSC so as to give them a majority on the Commission. Apparently it is up to employers to run training in Britain. This is at complete odds with the evidence presented in Chapter 12, which suggested that the existing MSC was itself deeply unhappy about the complacency shown by employers towards training. The evidence would suggest that, if you leave training only to employers, it just will not get done. Increasing the role of employers would also be the key for the trade unions to walk out of the Commission. Presumably the government would like this, but one of the strengths of the West German training system is that the trade unions are active supporters, backing up the tremendous concern shown by employers.

What all this suggests is a certain arrogance abroad in Whitehall. Ministers seem determined to ignore the lessons to be learnt from other countries, the warnings provided by their own officials, and the results even of official research. This is not surprising given that ministers are obviously not sympathetic to the idea that policy should be based on sound analysis and should above all be responsive to what the less-advantaged feel might be reasonable solutions to their problems. Unless the government learns how to tap into the hopes, fears and aspirations of those people who are on the margins of our society, our democracy will always remain seriously imbalanced.

Notes

1. Diocese of Liverpool, quoted on p. 169 of *Faith in the City* (1985).
2. We can only touch on this subject briefly. More detailed discussion is provided in Jones and Stewart (1985), Banham (1986) and Audit Commission (1987).
3. Audit Commission (1984).
4. Basing domestic rates on capital values was suggested by the Layfield Report (1976). This comprehensive study of the problems of local government finance was completely ignored by Government at the time and since.
5. Audit Commission (1987).
6. In Cleveland, this might imply creating an authority for Teesside, while Hartlepool declared UDI.

Bibliography

Anderson, J. *et al.* (1983) *Redundant Spaces*, Academic Press.
Armstrong, H. and Taylor, J. (1985) *Regional Economics and Policy*, Philip Allan.
Armstrong, H. and Taylor, J. (1986) *Regional Policy: The Way Forward*, Employment Institute, London.
Atkinson, A. and Micklewright, J. (1985) *Unemployment Benefits and Unemployment Duration*, London School of Economics, Suntory Toyota International Centre for Economics and Related Disciplines, London.
Atkinson, A. and Stiglitz, J. (1980) *Lectures on Public Economics*, McGraw-Hill.
Audit Commission (1984) *Impact on Local Authorities of the Block Grant Distribution System*, HMSO.
Audit Commission (1985) *Capital Expenditure Controls in Local Government in England*, HMSO.
Audit Commission (1986a) *Good Management in Local Government*, Local Government Training Board, London.
Audit Commission (1986b) *Managing the Crisis in Council Housing*, HMSO.
Audit Commission (1986c) *Improving Council House Maintenance*, HMSO.
Audit Commission (1986d) *Making A Reality of Community Care*, HMSO.
Audit Commission (1987) *The Management of London's Authorities: Preventing the Breakdown of Services*, Occasional Paper No. 2, HMSO.
Banham, J. (1986) 'Paying for Local Government', *Lloyds Bank Review*, July, No. 161.
Barnett, C. (1986) *The Audit of War*, Macmillan.
Bean, C., Layard, R. and Nickell, S. (eds) (1987) *The Rise in Unemployment*, Basil Blackwell.
Beaumont, P. (1976) 'The Operation of Assisted Labour Mobility Policy in a High Unemployment Region', Monograph prepared for the Manpower Services Commission.
Begley, M. (1986) 'The Unemployed Survey: Data on Occupations and Industry', Cleveland County Council, Information Note No. 315.
Berthoud, R. (1984) *The Reform of Supplementary Benefit*, Policy Studies Institute, London.

170

Bosworth, B. and Rivlin, A. (1987) *The Swedish Economy*, Brookings Institution, Washington.

Botham, R. (1984a) 'A Job Oriented Spatial Policy: The Case for Marginal Employment Subsidies', *Northern Economic Review*, No. 8, Winter.

Botham, R. (1984b) 'Employment Subsidies: A New Direction for Local Government Economic Initiatives', *Regional Studies*, Vol. 18.

Botham, R. and Lloyd. G. (1984) 'The Political Economy of Enterprise Zones', *National Westminster Bank Review*.

Brown, C. (1981) *Taxation and Labour Supply*, Cambridge University Press.

Buck, N., Gordon, I. and Young, K. (1986) *The London Employment Problem*, Oxford University Press.

Budd, A., Levine, P. and Smith, P. (1987) 'Long-Term Unemployment and the Labour Market: Some Further Results', London Business School, *Economic Outlook, 1986–1990*, Vol. 11, No. 5, February.

Burghes, L. (1987) *Made in the USA*, Unemployment Unit, London.

Burghes, L. and Stagles, R. (1983) *No Choice at 16: A Study of Education Maintenance Allowances*, Child Poverty Action Group.

Burton, J. (1987) 'Would Workfare Work?', Buckingham Employment Research Centre.

Carruth, A. and Oswald, A. (1986) 'Wage Inflexibility in Britain', London School of Economics, Centre for Labour Economics, Discussion Paper No. 258.

Caves, R. and Davies, S. (1987) *Britain's Productivity Gap*, National Institute of Economic and Social Research.

Champion, A. *et al.* (1987) *Changing Places: Britain's Demographic, Economic and Social Complexion*, Edward Arnold.

Charter for Jobs (1986) 'The Human Costs of Unemployment', *Economic Report*, Vol. 2, No. 1.

Cleveland County Council (1986a) *Cleveland's Unemployed: A Survey Report*, CR.547.

Cleveland County Council (1986b) *Survey of the Unemployed: Looking for Work*, CR.574.

Cleveland County Council (1986c) *Impact of Unemployment on Individuals, Families and Communities*, CR.573.

Cornwall, J. (1983) *The Conditions for Economic Recovery*, Martin Robertson.

Cowie, H., Emerson, R. and Harlow, C. (1984) *Rebuilding the Infrastructure*, Policy Studies Institute.

Dahrendorff, R. (1982) *On Britain*, British Broadcasting Corporation.

Daniel, W. (1974) *A National Survey of the Unemployed*, PEP XL, Broadsheet 54–6, London.

Davies, G. and Metcalf, D. (1985) 'Generating Jobs', *The Economics Analyst*, Simon and Coates, April.

Diamond, D., Pieroni, G. and Spence, N. (1984) 'Infrastructure and Regional Development: Research Review', London School of Economics, Geography Department, mimeo.

Dilnot, A. and Morris, C. (1983) 'Private Costs and Benefits of Unemployment: Measuring Replacement Rates', *Oxford Economic Papers*, Supplement, Vol. 35.

Economist Intelligence Unit (1982) *Britain's Jobless.*

European Commission (1986) *Third Party Financing Opportunities for Energy Efficiency in the European Community.*

Faith in the City (1985) The Report of the Archbishop of Canterbury's Commission on Urban Priority Areas, Church House Publishing, London.

Foord, J., Robinson, F. and Sadler, D. (1985) *The Quiet Revolution: Social and Economic Change on Teesside, 1965–1985*, British Broadcasting Corporation North-East, Newcastle.

Fothergill, S. and Gudgin, G. (1982) *Unequal Growth: Urban and Regional Change in the UK*, Heinemann.

Fothergill, S. *et al.* (1984) 'The Effect of Rates on Manufacturing Employment', Department of Land Economy, University of Cambridge, mimeo.

Garfinkel, I. and Palmer, E. (eds) (1978) *Creating Jobs*, Brookings Institution, Washington.

Green, A. and Owen, D. (1986) 'Long-Term Unemployment', Department of Employment, mimeo.

Green, A. *et al.* (1986) 'What Contribution Can Labour Migration Make to Reducing Unemployment?', in P.E. Hart (ed.) *Unemployment and Labour Market Policies*, Gower.

Gunby, D. (1984) 'Employment Subsidy Schemes — The Cleveland Experience', Liverpool Polytechnic, Seminar on Labour Market Policies and the Local Economy, 5 March.

Hakim, C. (1982) 'The Social Consequences of High Unemployment', *Journal of Social Policy*, Vol. 2, No. 4.

Hardman Report (1973) 'The Dispersal of Government Work From London', HMSO, Cmnd 5322.

Harrison, A. and Gretton, J. (eds) (1987) *Education and Training, UK 1987*, Policy Journals.

Hart, P.E. (ed.) (1986) *Unemployment and Labour Market Policies*, Gower.

Hausner, V.E. (ed.) (1986) *Critical Issues in Urban Economic Development*, Vol. 1, Clarendon Press.

Hillman, M. and Bollard, A. (1985) *Less Fuel, More Jobs: The Promotion of Energy Conservation in Buildings*, Policy Studies Institute, London.

Hughes, G. and McCormick, B. (1981) 'Do Council Housing Policies Reduce Migration Between Regions?', *Economic Journal*, Vol. 91.

Hughes, G. and McCormick, B. (1985) 'Migration Intentions in the UK: Which Households Want to Migrate and Which Succeed?', *Economic Journal*, Supplement, Conference Papers, Vol. 96.

Hughes, G. and McCormick, B. (1987) 'Housing Markets, Unemployment and Labour Market Flexibility in the UK', *European Economic Review*, No. 2.

Jackman, R. *et al.* (1986) *A Job Guarantee for Long-Term Unemployed People*, Employment Institute, London.

Johannesson, J. and Persson-Tanimura, I. (1978) *Labour Market Policy in Transition*, EFA, Swedish Ministry of Labour.

Jones, G. and Stewart, J. (1985) *The Case for Local Government*, 2nd edn, George Allen and Unwin.

Keeble, D. (1976) *Industrial Location and Planning in the United Kingdom*, Methuen.

Kirwan, R. (1986) *Local Fiscal Policy and Inner City Economic Development*, in V.A. Hausner (ed.) *Critical Issues in Urban Economic Development*, Vol. 1, Clarendon Press.

Kleineman, M., Pearce, B. and Whitehead, C. (1985) 'Housing: Twenty-Five Popular Fallacies', University of Cambridge, Department of Land Economy, Discussion Paper 14.

Lansley, S. and Mack, J. (1985) *Poor Britain*, George Allen and Unwin.

Layard, R. (1979) 'The Costs and Benefits of Selective Employment Policies: The British Case', *British Journal of Industrial Relations*, Vol. 17.

Layard, R. (1986) *How to Beat Unemployment*, Oxford University Press.

Layfield Report (1976) *Local Government Finance: Report of the Committee of Enquiry*, HMSO.

Leeming, R. (1986) 'Youth Self-Employment in Cleveland', Cleveland Youth Business Centre, mimeo.

Lever, W. and Moore, C. (eds) (1986) *The City in Transition: Policies and Agencies for the Economic Regeneration of Clydeside*, Oxford University Press.

Mays, N. and Bevan, G. (1987) *Resource Allocation in the Health Service: A Review of the Methods of the Resource Allocation Working Party (RAWP)*, Bedford Square Press/NCVO, London.

Metcalf, D. (1986) 'Labour Market Flexibility and Jobs', London School of Economics, Centre for Labour Economics, Discussion paper No. 254.

Moore, C. and Booth, S. (1986) 'Regional Economic Development in the North East: Critical Lessons from Scotland', *Northern Economic Review*, No. 14, Winter.

Moore, B. and Rhodes, J. (1976) 'A Quantitative Analysis of the Effects of the Regional Employment Premium and Other Regional Policy Instruments' in A. Whiting (ed.) *The Economics of Industrial Subsidies*, HMSO.

Morris, D. (ed.) (1985) *The Economic System in the UK*, 3rd edn, Oxford University Press.

National Audit Office (1987) *Department of Employment and Manpower Services Commission: Adult Training Strategy*, HMSO. ·

National Federation of Housing Associations (1985) *Inquiry into British Housing: Report*, National Federation of Housing Associations, London.

Nickell, S. (1986) 'The Government's Policy for Jobs: An Analysis' *Oxford Review of Economic Policy*, Vol. 1, No. 2.

Normington, D., Brodie, H. and Munro, J. (1986) *Value for Money in the Community Programme*, Manpower Services Commission/Department of Employment.

North, G. (1979) *Teesside's Economic Heritage*, Cleveland County Council.

Oswald, A. and Turnbull, P. (1985) 'Pay and Employment Determination in Britain: What Are Labour Contracts Really Like?', *Oxford Review of Economic Policy*, Vol. 1, No. 2.

Pahl, R. (1984) *Divisions of Labour*, Basil Blackwell.

Prais, S. *et al.* (1981) *Productivity and Industrial Structure*, Cambridge University Press.

Public Accounts Committee of the House of Commons (1986) 'Operation of the Rate Support Grant System', HMSO.

Rajan, A. (ed.) (1987) *Special Studies in the UK's Employment Prospects*, Butterworth.
Rajan, A. and Pearson, P. (eds.) (1986) *UK Occupation and Employment Trends in 1990*, Butterworth.
Regional Studies Association (1983) *Report on Inquiry into the Regional Problem in the UK*, Geobooks, Norwich.
Reynolds, D. and Sullivan, M. (1987) *The Comprehensive Experiment*, The Falmer Press, Cambridge.
Robinson, F. (1987) ' "It's Not Really Like That . . . ": Living With Unemployment in the North-East, 1987', British Broadcasting Corporation North-East, Newcastle.
Robinson, F. and Storey, D. (1981) 'Employment Change in Manufacturing Industry in Cleveland, 1965–76', *Regional Studies*, 15.
Roger Tym and Partners (1984) *Monitoring Enterprise Zones: Year Three Report*, Department of Environment.
Rutter, M. *et al.* (1979) *Fifteen Thousand Hours: Secondary Schools and Their Effects on Children*, Open Books, London.
Salomond, A. and Walker, J. (1986) 'The Oil Price Collapse: The Impact on the Scottish Economy', *Royal Bank of Scotland*.
Smith, S. (1986) *Britain's Shadow Economy*, Institute for Fiscal Studies/ Oxford University Press.
Standing, G. (1986) *Unemployment and Labour Market Flexibility: the UK*, International Labour Office.
Stern, J. (1986) 'Repeat Unemployment Spells; The Effect of Unemployment Benefits on Unemployment Entry', in R. Blundell and I. Walker (eds) *Unemployment, Search and Labour*, Cambridge University Press.
Storey, D.J. (1981) 'New Firm Formation, Employment Change and the Small Firm: The Case of Cleveland County', *Urban Studies*, 18.
Storey, D.J. (1982) *Entrepreneurship and the New Firm*, Croom Helm.
Storey, D.J. (1983) 'Regional Policy in a Recession', *National Westminster Bank Quarterly Review*.
Storey, D.J. (1985) *Manufacturing Employment Change in Cleveland, 1976–81*, Report commissioned by Cleveland County Council.
Storey, D.J. and Johnson, S. (1987) *Are Small Firms the Answer to Unemployment?*, Employment Institute.
Storey, D.J., Keasey, K., Watson, R. and Wynarczyk, P. (1987) *The Performance of Small Firms*, Croom Helm.
Therbörn, G. (1986) *Why Some People Are More Unemployed Than Others*, Verso, London.
Townsend, A.R. (1983) *The Impact of Recession: on Industry, Employment and the Regions, 1976–81*, Croom Helm.
Townsend, A.R. (1986) 'The Location of Employment Growth After 1978: the Surprising Significance of Dispersed Centres', *Environment and Planning*, A, Vol. 18, pp. 529–45.
Tyler, P., Moore, B. and Rhodes, J. (1986) *Geographical Variations in Costs and Productivity*, HMSO.
Wadhwani, S. (1985) 'Incomes Policies: The British Experience', London School of Economics, Centre for Labour Economics, Working Paper No. 761.

White, M. (1983) *Long-Term Unemployment and Labour Markets*, Policy Studies Institute.

Whiting, A. (ed.) (1976) *The Economics of Industrial Subsidies*, HMSO.

Wicks, M. (1978) *Old and Cold*, Heinemann.

Wiener, M. (1981) *English Culture and the Decline of the Industrial Spirit, 1850–1980*, Cambridge University Press.

Worswick, G.D.N. (ed.) (1985) *Education and Economic Performance*, Gower.

Index